DOING GOD'S WILL ON EARTH

LIVING
HISTORY

AN AUTOBIOGRAPHY OF
NORMAN M. "BUD" BYLSMA

EDITED BY
PETER J. BYLSMA

BYBLIO
PRESS
Inspire, Inform,
and Transform

To order this book, contact the Bylsma Foundation at the address or website below. Special discounts may be available on quantity purchases.

The Bylsma Foundation
11410 NE 124th Ave, #260
Kirkland, WA 98034
321-425-5757
www.bylsmafoundation.org

All revenue generated by the sale of this memoir will be channeled into the Bylsma Foundation, a non-profit tax-exempt organization. Its mission is to fund other nonprofit organizations that help people in need, promote justice in the world, seek and spread the truth, help others understand the stories and meanings of the Bible, and encourage those who need good news. Donations can be made to the Foundation through its website: www.bylsmafoundation.org.

The views expressed in this work are solely those of the author and do not necessarily reflect the views of the publisher, and the publisher hereby disclaims any responsibility for them.

Cover photo by Peter J. Bylsma (Bangladesh, 1981)

ISBN: 978-1-964060-27-9 (SC)
ISBN: 978-1-964060-26-2 (eB)

Library of Congress Control Number: 2025934725

CONTENTS

Section IV: U. S. Ministries

Appendixes

CONTENTS

Section IV: U. S. Ministries

Appendixes

FOREWORD

By Ray Bakke

"IF BY REASON OF STRENGTH,
THEY BE FOURSCORE YEARS…"
Psalm 90:10 (KJV)

The word fourscore, made famous by Lincoln's use of it in the Gettysburg Address, occurs some 32 times in the whole Bible, and in all but four cases, it refers to group numbers. In terms of age, it refers only to Abram, Isaac, Moses and Aaron, who were at least 80 or more years old. So Bud, I guess my most obvious fact is that biblically speaking, now that you are 80, you rounded out the big 5. How's that for seeing some theological significance to your basketball career?

I've had the privilege of reading the entire manuscript twice now, and I did so with even more amazement the second time, at the sheer range of experiences you had on the journey. But then we all know people who say that they have 60 years of experience, but under analysis, they really had one or two experiences 60 times. What is so impressive to me as a professor a decade behind you on the journey is that you modeled the action/reflection learning model long time before any of us read about it in "Pedagogy of the Oppressed" by a liberation theologian from Brazil.

I did have the privilege of intersecting with you in Chicago, Seattle, Bangladesh, and Portland. You co-created the Chicago Network, that support group that sustained me in that City for 28 years, and so I dedicated that book *Theology As Big As The City* to you and that group which taught me and sustained me in that city for nearly three decades. We also joint ventured consultations in Portland and Seattle, and Corean and I had the privilege of being hosted by you in Dacca as well. I've seen a spiritual consistency of motivation from vision, and a theology of hope in every period of your life, and this memoir makes that point obvious. People you nurtured and encouraged like the late Bill Leslie turned around and invested in me also. Your disciples and your sons have continued the legacy. You poured your life into a group of black men in Seattle, and one Harvey Drake is my doctoral student, and others are my colleagues in the city. Like the Kennedys, you worked hard and played hard. Imagine being "Benny the Bull" – it makes me think if you'd ever been in Young Life in San Diego, you'd have found a way to be the San Diego Chicken for the free tickets to some ball games.

Bud, you and your dear wife have paid your dues to more than two generations of kids across a continent and beyond. You invested in raising up local leaders, and I remember your bringing some of them to see me over the years. Like Jesus "*who chose 12 that he might be with them*", you have reminded us all that the incarnation is both our message and our model. *There is something to be taught in discipleship, but also something to be caught.* Jesus only had three years to change the world for all history, and he did it like you did, spending time with a few people and then moving on so you didn't stay to hover over and control them. You built relationships and gave them space. Well done my faithful friend.

A year ago, Dan Satterberg, now King County Prosecuting Attorney, stood a little back and apart from the graveside service of our mutual friend Norm Maleng with whom I'd grown up in Acme, Washington, and who for 28 years was clearly the most respected politician in Washington State, according to Police Chief Gil Kerlikowski. A big tear ran down his face, so I went to stand by him. Quietly, he said "Norm taught me at least one lesson every day over the 17 years I worked for him." What is he teaching you today," I asked. "Finish well" he said. Bud, that's what you are teaching people like me, and I'm grateful to God for every lesson I've learned from you.

Ray Bakke, a mere three score and ten, from Acme near Lynden where you came from.
Chancellor and Professor
Bakke Graduate University of Seattle
April 2008

PREFACE

In the last several years, while sharing bits of what I've experienced in these 80 years now, a number of people have said things like "you've lived more than a lifetime", **"write your memoirs"**, etc. They've encouraged me to pass on what certainly has been a lifetime so richly blessed of God. But I find it rather difficult to put much of that into something less than a huge volume, since Patti and I have had so many wonderful experiences together.

But the real reluctance in sharing my story comes from a strong sense of realizing my weaknesses… my failures… my limitations. For so many years I wasn't in touch with my insides, and was merely projecting onto my family that with which I grew up… **an inability to really love**… not providing at home a place of acceptance and affirming love. A strong work ethic, certainly… a lot of fun with the kids… yes… but weak on the heart level, disappointing to Patti in so many ways. So those areas of inadequacy as a husband and father… those things that I wish I could change about my past, have made me reluctant to want to put anything into print. But of course, I can't.

Having said that I also know how much I've experienced of God's **grace and love and forgiveness.** That is so overwhelming that while there is the sadness over whatever I wasn't as a person and for my family for many years (and I'm still not fully there), our Lord's forgiveness is so freeing that I am not encumbered with the past. What is most amazing to me is to see the many ways in which God has directed our lives… sometimes so clearly, at other times seeing it in retrospect. As I see it, history isn't really about us… or human events… it's about **God,** and His eternal purposes… it's really **HIS story**. (Hillary Clinton titled her autobiography *Living History,* so I'm merely plagiarizing… go ahead and sue, Hillary).

I am absolutely convinced that the many wonderful things that we've been allowed to be a part of were directly a result of God's generous and gracious hand… leading and guiding. So those unusual things in these pages are really **HIS** story, far more than mine. As I've reflected and gone through various of my past journals, I'm so overwhelmed and humbled at God's grace through the years… leading often when we didn't even know it, or compensating for my ignorance or stupidity. Truly **amazing grace!**

First will be my growing up years… no doubt a bit prosaic, but perhaps a bit of insight as to that which formed my insides. And while thirty of our years were with Young Life, the four years in Bangladesh were no doubt the most challenging, difficult and rewarding, so special focus will be given to those few years. But what a full and rich life we've enjoyed over four careers… and still looking forward to whatever is ahead.

In reviewing this, I note recurring **themes** throughout… risking… learning… strategy… change... community… the under-class… vision… mentors… culture and values…

decision-making… but overall, I trust **God's grace** and faithfulness.

I simply base all I believe and am on one central truth… that the **eternal Christ** alone provides a center… not for me only as an individual, but for all of history… and He will determine its end point… that **in Him is life in all its fullness**… and… **He has invited us to his party**, to celebrate life with Him!

EDITOR'S NOTE

Bud wrote this autobiography and distributed it to many of his friends who gathered in April 2008 at Bethany Presbyterian Church in Seattle, Washington to celebrate his 80th birthday. Copies were also sent to others throughout the country, and feedback from various readers who were in the ministry prompted him to ask me to publish his memoirs in book form. While he continued to be involved in discipleship and consulting activities for another decade, his work during that time is not included.

I edited this book with his permission and was in the process of finalizing it in Spring 2021 when he died. He had agreed to have an appendix added that summarized some of the noteworthy miracles that occurred in his life (see **Divine Interventions**) and were mentioned in his autobiography. I thought it was important to have these consolidated into one place where they could be easily found. They offer compelling proof of God's presence in his life.

Bud's writing style is so unusual that I decided not to have the publisher edit this book. He often used bold text for emphasis or to highlight an event or person, his frequent use of the ellipsis (…) was unconventional, and his misspelling were almost always intentional. I did minor editing and formatting of his memoirs prior to submitting it for publication, and I revised a tiny bit of text when clarification was needed. I also took the liberty to add a subtitle to the book: "Doing God's Will on Earth," for above all else, Bud wanted to do God's will everywhere he went. As a result, he led an unusual life for a person who stayed in the ministry for 65 years, often taking risks along the way, often changing locations and job responsibilities, always trying to speak words of wisdom, and always challenging others by using thought-provoking questions. He knew Jesus was always with him.

His memoirs reveal both his brilliance and his flaws as well as the lessons of his hard times and accomplishments. I have summarized his life in a **Postscript** at the end of this book. His life makes an excellent case study for those involved in any type of ministry, and putting this book on the internet free of charge (see Autobiography on his page of the Bylsma Foundation website, www.bylsmafoundation.org) enables all people throughout the world to learn from his experiences and insights for years to come. His 18 letters in the appendix provide many provocative insights and lessons that he learned during his years of ministry. To God be the glory!

Dr. Peter J. (Pete) Bylsma
(Bud's eldest son)
November 2024

Cradle To College

CHAPTER 1

A HEAD START?

Did it begin early?… finding creative ways to **"go for the gusto?"** As the older (by 5 minutes) of non-identical twins (an understatement), I ended up being taller and bigger than Pat, my twin brother. Was that from my crib assertiveness?

In 1988 Patti surprised me with a **"This Is Your Life"** 60th birthday dessert… people coming in from all over, and others writing thoughtful notes. For the occasion, my oldest brother, **Otto**, submitted the following:

"It was not by accident that Bud was always larger than his twin brother, Pat. When they were babies, our parents were concerned that Pat would start crying every night soon after they had been put to bed with their bottles. When the folks would go in to check, they would find Pat's bottle on the floor, empty, while Bud was still working away on his. So one night dad stuck around to see what was happening. Lo and behold, Bud emptied his bottle in no time at all, threw it on the floor, took Pat's bottle away from him, and proceeded to finish it too.

The cure didn't last very long. Soon Pat was crying again, but when the folks went in to check, Pat was sucking on an empty bottle, while Bud was still working away on his. The next night, dad saw what the problem was. He saw that Bud finished his bottle in record time, but instead of throwing his empty bottle on the floor as he had done before, he simply gave Pat his empty bottle and proceeded to finish off the bottle he had taken from Pat. Nuff said!"

Pat and I were born as the fifth and sixth **of seven children...** my parents had their hands full... but large families were not unusual in those days, especially among the Dutch. All four of my grand-parents came to America from Holland in the late 1800's... my father's parents to Iowa, my mother's to North Dakota. Then both families ended up in **Lynden**, **Washington**, where dad, **Charles**, met **Nancy Meenderinck...** married... and where most of us were born. Lynden... a small Dutch enclave, and where still today the largest building has the name across the top... **19 Bylsma 13**... a business my grandfather developed, and where dad worked. There is also a **"Bylsma Road"** just outside Lynden... and a **1927 Whatcom County** newspaper had a full page on my dad, as an outstanding businessman of the county.

So there was Otto John... Bernard Charles... Peter Francis (Percy, or **Perk**, as we called him)... Beulah Anne (**Boots**)... Norman Melvin (**Bud**)... Newman Marvin (**Pat)...** each about 2 years apart... and 9 years later came a surprise... Eleanor Jeanne.

Dad was rather amazing, both in business and intellect... a self-made man. After his army days in World War I he was chosen as **1 out of 10,000** by the government to go to college with all expenses paid, but for whatever reason, my mom said: "no, don't do that." Without ever going to college he learned **Greek** on his own, and would study the Bible regularly from the Greek text. He became an expert in drafting and blue-print reading… good enough that during the years of World War II he taught those to graduate students at the U. of Washington. In the early 40's he became **Boeing's chief trouble-shooter…** but, uncomfortable with internal politics, he quit. They tried to lure him back by continuing to pay him for 6 months… to no avail… and he ended up buying and selling real estate, eventually owning two large apartment buildings.

So different from our dad, who was bright, optimistic and playful, our mother was rather somber… legalistic. She passed on to dad any discipline… "just wait 'til your dad comes home, then he'll take care of you." So dad administered the spankings… on one occasion when he took Pat and me out to the woodshed, Pat put rocks in his back pockets to absorb the swats.

Much of our upbringing was very typical of the northern-European German/Dutch flavor, which was with limited emotional expression. I don't recall ever seeing my parents kiss, nor did I ever hear, to each other or to any of us, "I love you." **Dutch stoicism…** the church was of right doctrine, and great solemnity. But somehow dad knew there was more to Christianity than that, and feeling the need for new growth, he **moved to Seattle…** a brave move, though heavily criticized by his family. In those days no one left their roots and family and moved to the big city. Even today, almost all my relatives are still in Lynden (either under or above ground), and that's where both dad and mom are buried, and my brother Pete.

Did I inherit some of dad's restlessness with the status quo?... leaving our primary roots of rigid fundamentalism... knowing there was something more real and genuine out there? Some of my siblings felt I had gone way to the left... Young Life (YL) wasn't serious enough... and later, I had even become a **Presbyterian.** But it was in YL that I discovered the **Gospel of Grace**... very freeing, and so much deeper an understanding of the great truths of Scripture... grace, and not the legalism with which I was reared.

* * * * * * * * * *

Growing Up

Even after moving to Seattle when I was just a year old, we moved a lot... at one point moving to the house right next door, a larger home for the **9 of us.** We lived in the University District, and the UW campus became Pat's and my playground... I was put ahead twice in school, so ended up being a year ahead of him. At the age of 10 or 11 I got a job... **up every Friday at 4 a.m.,** delivering a weekly paper to every home in a 40 square block area. A year later I picked up a daily route, delivering the Seattle Star to about 25 customers, which led to having a paper 'stand' on University Way and 42nd... every afternoon and Saturdays, selling the 3 daily newspapers on the corner. I did well enough that they gave me the corners of 43rd and 47th, 2 of the 3 prime corners.

I never owned a bike until the 8th grade... we were too poor. One Christmas Pat and I were given a wagon... mainly so we could go to the alleys behind the stores on University Way to pick up discarded wooden boxes and crates, which became firewood for heating our home. At other times we would take our wagon down under the University bridge, where railroad cars would unload coal, and we would pick up the coal that had spilled onto the ground… more fuel for our stove at home.

Almost all clothes were hand-me-downs… I don't remember ever getting anything new, though I may have. But it was just natural to inherit what came down via 3 older brothers, and we never thought a thing of it. I recall dad putting cardboard inside the sole of my shoes when they wore a hole, and then he purchased some "Solo", a tar-like substance that would be spread on to the sole of the shoe… the shoemaker was too expensive. Those were the early-mid 30's… the **Great Depression years**… tough on everybody, and yet I don't recall ever thinking of us as being poor. Each of us had assigned chores, both indoors and out, and we all learned the meaning of hard work.

My folks moved to Riverton, just south of Seattle, so dad could be closer to Boeing. Some of the relationships there were difficult for me… Roy Quealy, same class as I, but 4 inches shorter and 20 pounds lighter, was always bullying me… but I was afraid of getting into any sort of real fight. He even said once "you're bigger and stronger than I, and could pound me if you wanted to, but **you're chicken.**" He was right. He had a girlfriend, Myrna, who decided she liked me better, so left him for me. One day after I walked her home from school, Roy and a friend of his stopped me on my way home and beat me up pretty badly, leaving me in a ditch. Tough neighborhood.

At Foster Hi there were annual "**Smokers**", an evening of high-school-aged boxing. In P.E. classes we had boxing instruction, so Pat and I agreed to be in that year's Smoker… 3 rounds of 1 minute each. Unfortunately, it was rather one-sided, as my greater weight and size was just too much for him. They thought I was pretty good, so for the next Smoker, 6 months later, they matched me with a classmate who was much heavier than I. But of course I would be quicker, and quite capable… **Wrong!** I was **pummeled**… and I'm sure Pat watched with glee.

One Sunday… family at the dining room table… radio on… when, **"we interrupt this program with a special report… this morning Pearl Harbor was bombed"**… December 7, 1941. The war changed many things very quickly, and there was concern that, being near Boeing, we could be bombed. So at night the entire city would have very few lights on, with all shades drawn, to reduce great amounts of light from a metro area. **Gas rationing** went into effect, with everyone receiving either an A, B or C sticker. **A** -- 4 gallons a week… **B** — a bit more, if engaged in critical war effort… which dad was, as a Boeing employee. We almost never saw a **C**… unlimited gas, for high officials.

It wasn't long after that we moved back to Seattle, and I was a 2nd semester freshman at Roosevelt Hi… went out for baseball that spring, but with every pitch I stepped back 3 feet… **scaredy cat.** I always worked during my school years, and the summer of '42 I went to work on my cousin's farm, 4 miles from Lynden… $15 a month, and room and board. He liked what I was doing, so I asked my folks if I could stay on, and I went to Lynden Hi that fall semester, milking 7-8 cows **by hand,** both morning and evening… plus the other chores needed on a farm.

Back to Seattle for the second sophomore semester, I got a job as a janitor in a school, 3 hours a day, **75 cents an hour**. Pat was working at Buchan Bakery, and through him I got a job there… **50** cents an hour. But it would mean **8** hours on Saturday, plus full time in the summer, and I felt I'd get paid sooner… by summer I was at **$1** an hour. One of my jobs was washing the trucks, which meant driving them to the garage. On my 16th birthday I drove a truck to take my driving test… to get my driver's license… no problem. I ended up working at the bakery, in various jobs, through my first year of college.

School was **fun**, but classes were of little interest to me. Even though I was the champion speller in junior hi, I was never motivated to study. In four years of high school I had **two A's**… one in **P.E.,** and one in **typing** (best class I ever took to prepare for the world of computers)… and flunked woodshop twice, from just dinking around. There were 3 lunch periods, and I had woodshop class during the first and second lunch periods. So I would go to class… have roll taken… and then skip out and have all 3 lunch periods… fun, but after a couple of weeks the teacher said: "you can have all 3 the rest of the semester." I rarely brought home any school assignments, and really had no interest in studying. I genuinely regret that, and even today I do not consider myself a well-educated person … not having wanted to pursue studies in the arts, classics, etc. (As they say… the 4 best years in a Dutchman's life?… 1st grade.)

I was always fairly good in athletics… usually the first person chosen in pick-up games… in the 7th grade I **beat the 8th grader** in handball for the school championship. The frequent school changes meant I didn't enter the routine in going out for sports, so I helped start a city league basketball team at the bakery where I was working. But my senior year I was encouraged to go out for the basketball team at Roosevelt Hi, and we played for the city championship. The next year our coach went to the **University of Washington** as head basketball coach, and, much to my surprise, **he offered me a full ride. Wow!** But of course mom said that would mean being at that '**worldly**' UW, and I shouldn't go there.

So in 1945 off I went to Simpson Bible Institute **(SBI)...** a 3-year school of training especially for missions and church work. At that time there was no such thing as government student loans, so I worked both during the school year and in the summers... one summer in a logging camp in Montana... slept in a tent... and was fully self-supporting from the day I left high school.

How many times I've reflected on what would have happened if I had gone to the UW to play basketball... what different route would my life have taken? (In later years I ended up playing against both Wilt Chamberlain and Kareem Abdul Jabbar, and worked out with the pros in Baltimore when we lived there.) How different would my life have been? But I realize that had I gone to the UW, I would have missed out on having a life that has been so incredibly rich and rewarding... I don't regret for a minute what I did, and **grateful for how God uses misguided rationale for His purposes.** And, as I was to see on later occasions... that's the nature of a God who at times overrules, or broadens, our limited perspectives.

CHAPTER 2

COLLEGE YEARS

SBI had never had a basketball team, so that first year I asked the men's Dean for **$100** so we could buy a couple of balls, and uniforms. We didn't have a gym, so practiced once a week in a church gym about two miles away, and where we played some of our games… mostly against church teams. But the second year we played some college freshman teams, a couple of junior colleges and **Seattle Pacific College's varsity.** Expectedly, they trimmed us, **but the next year… we beat them**… it really was David slaying Goliath… and they offered me a scholarship.

The summer after my 2nd year at Simpson I chauffeured the President on his annual trip to California … stayed at the home of a lady in Sherman Oaks, who told me of this charming, attractive brunette who would be coming to Simpson from there, and would I be of help in having her feel welcomed. So in September, when a group arrived from Sherman Oaks, I took my dad's big Packard to pick them up at the Greyhound station. I didn't see any '**attractive brunette**' among the group, and while driving them to the school I asked: **"didn't Patti Barber come with you?"** Whereupon they said: **"yes, she's right here**

in the back seat"… (foot in mouth disease). She was bundled up in this huge fur coat kind of thing, with a big mop of hair.

Neither of us was impressed with the other, but I dutifully wanted to be of help… and, there was a charm she had. One evening while walking back to school with a group on a Sunday night, she and I were behind the others, and I took her hand… **bold move**. Then when she was going home for Christmas, we were alone in the bookstore, and I gave her a kiss… **on the forehead! Bolder move!!** The second semester we were more or less dating, but I knew that my folks weren't too keen on that… she wasn't Dutch… so when she went back to California in May, I wasn't sure I'd see her again.

For some reason, I was interested in going to **Nyack**, a 4-year sister school of Simpson… and, as I recall, it would be sort of an adventure… **New York!** But I didn't receive an acceptance from Nyack, and SPC was still working on their scholarship funding. I waited… and waited… so finally I told the Lord that **whichever acceptance came first**, that's where I felt He would want me to go. One **morning** the mail brought the acceptance from Nyack… and then **that afternoon** I got a call from SPC, giving the **ok** on a scholarship. Was there any question?… no. On to Nyack.

However, Patti and I communicated during the summer… so I decided that I would go to Nyack **via Los Angeles**, to see her. I sent a trunk of clothes and misc. on ahead to Nyack, then **hitch-hiked to L.A.,** and we had 3 days together… I was hooked. I then **hitch-hiked to N.Y.** (7 **rides in 3 days**… put **N.Y.** in white tape on my black suitcase), and we wrote each other every other week for the entire school year. Having dated quite a bit earlier at Simpson, much to my surprise, I wasn't interested in dating any gal back there. The only direct contact Patti and I had all year was when I phoned her at Christmas time... **on a pay phone. We talked until the nickels filled up the box.** The next June I hitch-hiked back to L.A... this time **22** rides in 3 days... had 3 days with Patti, then hitch-hiked back up to Seattle.

I entered Seattle Pacific as a junior (yes, squeezed 4 years into 6... rare those days). Patti was back at Simpson, but I was still not sure about her... so while there on one occasion I asked their Dean of Men about several gals... and then about Patti, and he said: **"she's a flamingo in a chicken coop."** Wow... could I let a flamingo go??? We got engaged New Year's eve, 1949. But we couldn't afford to get married, since I still had another year at Seattle Pacific, so she said: "I'll not go on to finish college, I'll work," so that's what she did.

We have both been rather bemused over the years as to how two persons, **both so immature** and so different in most every way, could end up together. Neither of us had the slightest idea of what marriage really meant, or was all about. I was a meat and potatoes Dutchman, while her recent years were in '**society**' with her grandparents. The first time I was going to meet them in Los Angeles, she clued me in... **"you don't say 'hello,' you say 'how do you do.'"** They were very opposed to our getting married, and when her granddad sent me a letter, **"7 reasons why you shouldn't get married"...** I wrote him back with **7 reasons why we should,** including that I was the proud owner of a car... a 1929 Nash convertible... (a real beauty... 23,000 miles... for which I paid $85.) So we were married **June 9, 1950**, the week after she graduated from Simpson. I bought her wedding gown material, and she sewed it... she was an excellent seamstress.

One area of difference of the two of us… Patti was **a very good student**… and quietly bright. Later on, when we were living in Southern California, she decided to go back to school. At Biola College she was taking 12 hours of classes one quarter… and **got straight A's.** She had 3 years to go, so I suggested that she **take 20 hours**, not study any more than with the 12 hour load, **and get B's**… so that's what she did. With 2 teenagers in high school, plus two younger children… for 2 straight years she took 20 hours of classes each quarter… and **got all A's** but one… graduating from college **magna cum laude**… the same week Cherie graduated from high school. **Smart woman!**

* * * * * * * * * *

I was now in my senior year, and Patti was working at a bank. YL had invited me to come on Student Staff ($50 mo.), so… I was leading a YL club… taking a full load of classes… playing basketball… later in the year started a **2nd** club from scratch **(how dumb can I be?)**… all while being newly married. (Early signs of **workaholism**?… avoidance of intimacy?). I had switched my major twice… started in **Philosophy**, but concluded that all philosophers ask the same questions, but come up with different answers… so, how do we know what's true?… it seemed so subjective. So I switched to a **History** major… and when in the third quarter I took a course in **Anatomy**, I loved it, and switched again. So in the Fall, as a senior and now a **Physiology major**, I had almost all science classes, taking 400 level courses, such as Kinesiology, while also taking Biology 101 alongside freshmen.

Fortunately I had a good faculty advisor. One of the courses I took was Parasitology, a 1 credit course… I was the only student. So he told me to get the book, read it, and come in for the final on the last day of winter quarter… which would be in his office at **9:00 p.m.** On that last day I had still not read the book (never let studies interfere with your education), and that evening I was refereeing a basketball game. So during half-time I thumbed through the book, looked over the Table of Contents, and from page 1 memorized the definition of Parasitology. When I arrived in his office he asked me if I was ready, and I told him I was. He said: **"Give me a definition of Parasitology"…** whereupon I recited it perfectly. He turned to his assistant and said: **"give him a B."** He knew me.

We lived in a small two-room apartment near the school… when suddenly, to our surprise, we discovered Patti was pregnant. That summer, I had to take **20 hours of classes** in order to graduate, all **in a 4 week session** … and, **had to get 4 A's** to bring my GPA up to **qualify** for graduation.

What a wild summer of '51. We lived in the lovely home of Dr. Thompson… the world's expert on salmon… while he and his wife were in Alaska. Since Patti was expecting soon, she couldn't work now, so I worked at **2 jobs.** I would leave for work each evening at 7:30 for an office janitorial job, 8-11:30… then to a can factory, working midnight to 7:30 a.m.… **then 4 classes, 5 days a week,** straight through from 7:45 to 12:15. Home for lunch, then to bed… up at 7 p.m., to eat and go to work… straight for 4 weeks. I would study during 'lunch hours' (**3-3:30 a.m.**)**,** and on the week-ends. The amazing thing… in one class of 45 students I got the **top grade**, and overall got **3 A's** and 1 B… short of the necessary GPA, but they said ok, and '**conferred**' a B.S. And, that month **Cherie Lynn** was born… wild days for Patti.

A Young Life Career

CHAPTER 3

EAST COAST

That summer Young Life invited me to come on staff, and Norm Robbins, who initially got me involved and had moved to Philadelphia, asked if I would come there. This sounded great, and I became 1 of 7 new staff in the first training program YL ever had. Jim Rayburn, YL's Founder, wanted new staff to learn under some of the top Christian scholars in the country, so arranged that we would **go to where the professors were**... we called it the **Station Wagon University.**

Our initial time would be 2 weeks of orientation in **Colorado**... then we'd go to **Pasadena** for 2 weeks at **Fuller Seminary**. So I drove to Colorado, while Patti and Cherie flew to **Los Angeles**, so they could be there with her granddad. After the time at Fuller we drove back to Colorado for another week of classes with a visiting prof, and then, in the midst of an early November snowstorm, Patti, Cherie and I ventured out for **Philadelphia.** I had made a bed from an orange crate for 4-month old Cherie, which would hang over the back of the front seat... easier for Patti to tend her while en route.

What a wild trip in that **'38 Olds**... cold and snowy much of the way. On the Pennsylvania Turnpike (in those days the only super hi-way in the country) Cherie was wanting her bottle, so I stopped by the side of the Turnpike, took a small pan we had, and drained some hot water from the bottom of the radiator, so we could warm her bottle in it... such a new world for Bud and Patti.

We arrived in Philadelphia, and Norm had arranged a house rental for us... furnished. We were eager to see it, what with the exotic address: **1 Circle Lane**, Norwood, Pennsylvania. It proved to be slightly **less** than exotic... 4 rooms, and a 'basement'... you could see daylight through the walls... with a coal furnace, which I had to learn how to stoke, to keep it going all night. The furniture was so bad that a year later when we moved the Salvation Army wouldn't take it.

One of the first things I had to do was join the others in the Station Wagon U for a couple of weeks in Long Island, then on to New Jersey, with **Dr. Larry Kulp,** (founder of the **Carbon 14** method of dating matter), then on to Philadelphia... where we lived for 9 days with, and in the home of, **Dr. Donald Gray Barnhouse**, one of the leading pastor/theologians in the country. What a rare experience, to live with one of the giants of the Faith, and watch how he lived and studied. But the most memorable time occurred on a Saturday.

Dr. Kulp hadn't finished in his time with us... **Science and Scripture...** so Dr. Barnhouse arranged for him to come to his home. He sat in on the lecture, and then began to question Dr. Kulp in certain areas. Here was a world class scientist being challenged by a top drawer theologian... and for 5 hours the 7 of us sat in utter amazement, listening to two giants candidly interact in deep dialog. At the end Dr. Barnhouse asked Dr. Kulp if he could come to his summer session on **Earth Science** to learn more of the congruency of science and Scripture. What a humble giant. This occasion was one of many through the years, in which I had the privilege of having exposure to leading men and women... people who helped shape my life and how I think. I concluded later that perhaps we **learn more from people than from books.**

On that trip, between Long Island and New Jersey, the engine of my trusty Olds blew. I still owed $150 on it, so now... little furniture, debts, no car... but somehow we weren't worried. Norm had an old junker I could use, but then I bought another... of course more debt. We moved to Newtown Square the next year, and the evening of **December 25th** we went in to Philadelphia to see the **Harlem Globetrotters** play... **seats high up in the arena... lots of stairs.** A ton of laughs, but some strenuous walking... and at **6 a.m. the next morning Peter James was born**.

Through the years God has done so many wonderful things for us, and one of those early times was the next summer. We were going to Seattle, but had to rent our apartment in order to have the money to go. The morning we had to leave it still **hadn't been rented**, but then a man called and said he saw an ad in a paper **2 weeks earlier**, and asked if the apartment was still available. We said **"yes"...** he came over... **paid 2 months rent... and we drove off** an hour later.

* * * * * * * * * *

Baltimore

Those 3 years in Philadelphia were not easy for me, as Norm operated by the seat of his pants, and I felt I mostly learned what **not** to do. When in 1954 the situation arose to start YL in Baltimore, I was eager to take that, so now I was on my own. We lived in one of those 'row houses', attached for the entire block, in which most people in the Baltimore area live. Much went fairly well, but YL nationally was not solid financially... **one month I got a check for $17**... another month for **$0**... yes, an actual check. So Jim Rayburn asked everyone in the country to get a job, and I ended up driving city buses. One of the men at our church offered me a job making 2-3 times my YL salary, and I asked myself**... if money were no problem, what would I do**? It was not a difficult thing, as I simply said to myself that I'd do exactly what I'm doing... and I've never looked back. I loved what I was doing, and YL had enriched our lives so greatly.

Soon after came another one of those times when **God came alongside.** One evening we had dinner... quite aware that it was the end of our food... and we just gave thanks for what we had. We told no one, and there would be virtually nothing for breakfast. The next morning, when I went out to get the newspaper from the front porch... there sat 4-5 boxes of groceries. Again, we had told no one... what **faith-building times.**

One Christmas we had little funds, and I was hoping to buy a Christmas tree... those days a really good one cost about $5. I saw one I really liked, and told the guy I liked that one... but only had $2, and wanted to **get a tree for a poor lady and her**

2 children. He said ok… so I paid him the $2 and took the tree home… to a poor lady and her 2 children.

The summer of 1955 I had taken a busload of kids to Frontier Ranch in Colorado, and while playing a basketball game my knee went **POP!!!!** When I got back home I had to have it operated on, and when they got in there, it was somewhat complicated… so the question from the doctor was "are you going to be playing professional basketball, or not?" I had worked out with the Bullets and other pros… but knew that was probably not in my future, so I told them "no"… but as a result I've lived with a bum knee ever since.

Baltimore was not a fun place to do YL, as teenagers could go to any school they wanted in the city… thus no community school spirit. So we focused on the suburbs, and things went quite well. It was my first experience in developing both a Committee, and leadership training, and I found I really enjoyed it. Then I started a club in **Annapolis,** which was **35** miles away. That was also the year that **m/m's were introduced,** .05 cents a package. There were **34 m/m's in a package**, so I would have **1 each mile**… still haven't kicked the habit.

Salaries in YL were on the thin side, and we owned virtually nothing, so how do I establish credit? **Idea**… with the help of a local Committeeman, I **borrowed $500** from a bank… **but never used it**, and 4 months later paid it all back. Then 6 months later I borrowed **$1000,** and did the same… didn't use it… then paid it back. Now we had good credit… valuable down the road.

Bob Patton, who we had known from our Philadelphia days, was now in a D.C. suburb, and he encouraged me to start YL in Wheaton Hi, the school near him. So we took two guys to camp in Colorado... both key in different ways. John was loud and known by everyone, and Jay was an intellectual... **so we had a mouth and a brain**. We began club in the spring of '57, and it got off to a good start... about 25 kids. So now I was running **3** YL clubs... one in **Towson**, where we lived (northern suburb of Baltimore)... one in **Annapolis**... and one near **D.C.**... each of the latter two about 35 miles from home. In **1955** I bought a new **Chevy Belair**, and one year later, with **43,000** miles on it (and that was before freeways), I traded it in for a new one. (I was saving the world... just look at my odometer.)

Every Tuesday that school year of '57-'58 I would **leave home at 6 a.m.** and drive to Wheaton... 7:00 a.m. campaigners (YL's 'follow-up') with a group of guys (2 of them ended up with YL). After that I'd have breakfast at the Patton's, then head downtown to meet with individuals and discover the city... often spent time at the **Library of Congress**, reading and studying... then in the afternoon I'd go to the school for contacts. During basketball season the coach gave me a uniform and a locker, so I could work out with the team... at practice I would play the role of the center of the next team they were playing, and of course this gave me a great in with the athletes... many were now coming to club.

After dinner (at the Patton's) we had club... then from **9-10 p.m.** I had **leadership training** for about a dozen who had become interested in getting involved. So I **got home around 11:30 p.m.**... long days, but solid groundwork was being laid for initiating YL in D.C.

The 4 years in Baltimore weren't fun… but God gave us **2 gifts** there… **Philip Jon, and Stephen Scott.**

* * * * * * * * * *

The Capital and the Crisis

By now all areas in YL had to become self-supporting, so the question was… how could we get enough interest and funding to get **YL** going **in D.C.?** During that year of driving weekly from Baltimore I had formed a Committee of 5 men, and suggested a plan. The venerable **Dr. Richard Halverson** (Pastor at 4th Presbyterian, and later Chaplain to the Senate… who had included me in his 'group of 12') would help in getting a mailing list… we ended up with a list of **500.** We mailed a **post card** once a week, each with some facet of YL… **contact, club, campaigners, camps,** etc. At the bottom of each card was **"The Washington area needs Young Life."** The last mailing was an invitation to a YL dinner, featuring **Dick Halverson, Jim Rayburn, Senator Hatfield**, et al.

I knew that the only way to start in a new city was to convince Jim Rayburn, and that there had to be adequate community support. So at the same time as weekly cards were going to 500 people, I had each of the 5 Committeemen rotate in writing a letter to Jim Rayburn… so **he would get a letter every week**. By the time he came for the dinner he had received more than a dozen letters… and he told me he had **never seen a city so eager for YL**… didn't realize it was only **5 people** who had written. We raised almost an entire year's budget that evening… Jim said **"go"**… and the summer of '58 we moved to Silver Spring, Maryland, just on the north edge of D.C.

Our years there were great, with such good friends... many with whom we still stay in close touch. Clubs started in both Maryland and Virginia, and in 1959 I laid out a vision of **1000 kids in clubs in 5 years**. One of the more challenging clubs I ever started was at Montgomery-Blair Hi in Silver Spring, a prominent school in the area. We had one gal go to camp in Colorado... the right one... popular and a real leader. She got many of the football team to come that first night, and we elected **Mike Sheplee** as president. When he got home he told his mother he wasn't going back to '**that thing**', but she said he had to, since he was elected president.

Mike was a rugged lineman, one of the football players who, as a team, **broke six legs of opponents that year**. It was one of the most difficult groups I'd ever worked with... at times meeting in a smoke-filled room, gals on guys laps, etc. Before club I'd drive around the block, hoping I'd get hit by a truck... but praying along the way. (When Patti and I were first married, we were considering a missions career, and thought maybe we'd do YL first for a few years. Early on a veteran missionary told us **"you're doing as difficult mission work as anyone overseas... maybe more so, in working with indifferent and pagan teenagers"**... YL was essentially a **ministry to non-Christians**.)

During that year Mike never said a word at club, but his presence brought others. In the spring we had a weekend camp at a hotel in Ocean City, and a bunch of these guys went. They decided to stay up all night... to which I said: "ok, but you don't leave your rooms." The next week, just before club Mike asked if he could say something, and I thought... oh no, he's going to talk about the big bash and all-nighter at camp. But in the middle of our singing, he just sat down on the piano bench and said to the rest: **"you know, we've been coming to club all year, listening to Bud… and tonight when he talks, you listen."** That's all he said… blew me away. I met with him a couple of days later and learned he had trusted the Lord, and we began meeting regularly after that.

It had been a great start in D.C., but early September of **1960** I came down with **meningitis and encephalitis**… paralyzed from the chest down, and rushed to the hospital. A few evenings later, Wheaton club kid Bill Ingram came to visit me after they had the first club of the new school year… "hey Bud, **over 100 kids in club tonite.**" I told him "impossible, I wasn't there"… just kidding, of course… but it was an indicator of what God was doing in the ministry in the whole area.

Toward the end of that first week in the hospital, someone came to tell me that **Mike Sheplee** had just been wheeled in downstairs… **dead on arrival**, from a car accident. A couple of days later my doctor said I could go to his 'wake,' where I ran into his mother, Sylvia. She rushed up to me and cried **"Oh Bud… why, why, why?"** I softly told her that Mike had given his life to God… and then, as God does at special times, He gave me words… and I spoke of Jim Elliot's book *Shadow of the Almighty,* in which he virtually alludes to his own early death… **"God is inhabiting eternity with people, and I must not limit him to just old people"**… that obviously Mike was special to Him, and chose to bring him to Himself when he was still young. She felt very consoled… weeping, yet feeling a deep sense of gratitude. (Someone once said that each of us should have something to look forward to in death… and one of those special things for me will be to see Mike again.)

After a week or so in the hospital, I was required to be in isolation… no mental activity… **no visitors, no television, no newspapers**, etc. So an elderly couple had me come to stay in their home down on the Potomac River. Several days later Dick Halverson came over one afternoon to tell me that **my father had died the day before**. Wow! I wasn't ready for that, and not in an emotional or mental state to handle it. Nor could I go to **Seattle** for the funeral… or even be with my family 30 miles away… I was **alone**. But an amazing thing happened, which I've recalled often and so clearly

That very night… one of those nights as dark as the inside of a black cat… I lay there, weeping… the entire night… and felt so alone. I suddenly became aware of something almost surreal. Even though I couldn't see my own hand if I reached out, I became incredibly aware of the presence of Jesus… it was as if I reached out, **I would touch him.** In the midst of perhaps the greatest crisis of my life, **I** had such a **deep sense of real peace, of deep joy**… it was wonderful… even though at the same time I was feeling such deep sorrow. What I concluded later was… the reality of knowing God not as intellectual truth… in correct theological assertions… but in a relationship that was so personal and real… that at the time when I most needed **love**… **comfort… joy… hope…** I didn't experience those. **What I experienced was a person**, and that when I need love… or hope… or joy… or comfort… or whatever… what **God gives** is not those, but **Himself**… that **He embodies each of those**. What a great lesson for me.

After several weeks the doc said I had to be away from home for a period, so I went to Obie Snider's farm up near **Altoona, PA**. During my last year in Philadelphia I had driven the 200 miles every other week for about 4 months to help him start a YL club. He was an incredible farmer… Wheaton College grad… and one year was named 'national farmer of the year.' He had an office in his barn that was as nice as our living room, so I was able to stay there, where he had a hide-a-bed.

With the encephalitis, **I was sleeping 16 hours a day,** so I'd arise mid-morning, have breakfast, then go out in the woods… shoot small game… and do whatever I could to while away the tedium until early to bed. Then the doctor said I had to be **at least 500 miles** away from my work **for a year,** and… that we **couldn't have all 4 kids with us.** By now it's early December, so we had some hard decisions to make.

(An interesting note here… one of our YL Committee men was regional manager for Lincoln-Mercury, and he arranged for me to purchase a **new** Mercury station wagon for **40% below dealer's cost…** the out-going 1960 model. But in a ministry supported by friends, I just didn't feel comfortable in driving a big, expensive car, so I asked Dick Halverson for advice… to which he said "for those who like you, it won't make any difference… for those who don't like you, it won't make any difference." I bought it.)

We decided that I would drive to Seattle in our new wagon with Cherie and Pete, and Patti would fly to Palo Alto to be with her grandparents… and good friends from Philadelphia took Phil (4), and Steve (2) for an indefinite period. Then right after Christmas Cherie, Pete and I drove to Palo Alto from Seattle. We rented a home near the Stanford University campus, stocking our home with furniture from Goodwill and garage sales, and soon the doctor told me to get a job. I applied and was accepted for a job in personnel at Lockheed, but the doctor said **"sorry, brawn, not brain"...** so began my career as a **pickle factory worker**. I was promoted from unloading pickles... to the assembly line... to making brine for sweet pickles... to working the fork lift (dropped a whole fork lift of empty bottles on the street)... went to being 3ʳᵈ from the top... all in 6 months... (**what talent!**)

In March the doctor said Phil and Steve could join us, and some friends flew them to Los Angeles, so I flew down there to bring them up to Palo Alto... so good to be together again.

By mid-summer the doctor said **I could return to YL...** but since so much was uncertain during the year about my future, YL had decided to bring another person for Washington, D.C. **I was just crushed,** as we all loved it there, and I had had great hopes for what was ahead... but down deep I knew they couldn't wait. So now I was delighted that I could at least get back to what I loved. YL gave me several options, one of which was **San Jose...** where they had **2 clubs, averaging 20 each**. Since I enjoy a challenge, that's where I said we would go.

We tried to purchase a home, but no bank would consider us... inadequate income. Finally one bank said ok... on the basis of **10 years with one employer**. I flew back to D.C., sold the home to the family who had been renting it, and then purchased a new car... this time the out-going model at **20%** below dealer's cost... (you know me and cars... my most recent one was my 62nd)... drove back to San Jose, in 3 days.

West of Salt Lake City and before entering Nevada is a straight stretch of highway... not a turn for 50 miles or more. I was doing about **85**, and then noticed lights in my rear view mirror... gaining on me. I had driven this road several times, and in the distance ahead I could see the lights of that town I knew was in **Nevada**. I thought... I'll get out of Utah before he catches me... so I pushed it up to **105.** But before long, those lights ahead still seemed so far away... and the lights in my mirror were getting closer. So I slowed back down to 85... wasn't going to get a ticket going over 100. Just a few minutes later this car came whizzing by... passing me... **an old Nash**... I thought I was in neutral. Whew!

CHAPTER 4

CALIFORNIA YEARS

San Jose

Our 5 years in San Jose were highly productive in almost every way. We developed a strong leadership-training program, and when a new club started, I would meet with that leader each week. The most difficult part of leading a YL club is in giving the message... primarily **what** to speak on, and then **how** to deliver it. So I'd give each new leader his club talk each week... have it taped, listen to it the next day, then go over it with him and give him the next week's talk. By the end of the year they'd be able to do it well on their own.

I had brought **Sandy Vitullo** from the East... she had moved from Philly to D.C. to work with us there... good with kids, and great in the office. In our third year, one day Sandy said to me... **"look Bud, last week there were more than 1000 kids in clubs."** I remember thinking "Lord, aren't you funny"... that was the 5-year goal I had set in **1959 in D.C.,** and here we are, right on time... only in a different city. Now we had **12 clubs,** averaging close to **100 each.** Everything was going so well, with almost 30 volunteer leaders, and a strong Committee.

My first experience with 'urban' was when I decided to take some kids from the city to our urban camps in Colorado. I talked with the local authorities, and got **3 boys... wards of the court...** told them it would cost them **$5** to go to camp. When I picked up Charles Simpson at 7:00 a.m., his mother came to the door and I reminded her of the $5. She disappeared into the **other** room of the house, and I heard this piggy bank being shaken, until I heard no more jingling. Then she came to the door, and said: **"would $4.78 be ok?"** Each of the 3 had a little bag, and with luggage for 4 of us... for a 10 day trip... the trunk of my car was only about half full. It was a life-changing time for all of us, and **my first step toward the less-advantaged.**

But after several years in San Jose **I began to sense something I hadn't anticipated**. Our experience back east was that of seeing many kids come to the Lord, and then watching them grow... and grow... in their faith. What I saw here was a lot of kids responding to the Gospel, but there was a leveling off after a while. Being an analytical sort of person, I couldn't figure that out... but others had said that was their observation also.

My conclusion, right or wrong, was that so many families were **transplants to California** from out of state... that those in the East had stronger extended family ties, and deeper roots... giving kids a greater personal identity, and more stability.

So then in 1965 YL President Bill Starr spoke at a regional staff conference, and a comment he made struck me so strongly... **"I don't believe in 'total commitment', I believe in the offered life."** I thought ... how many times have we heard things like "He's either Lord of all, or not Lord at all"... or "are you fully surrendered"... or..., and we do so much naval gazing to determine if we're 'totally committed.' What Bill said seemed to make so much sense... the **offered life.** That really rang a bell, and I recall so clearly saying to the Lord**... "here's my life... offered to you... warts and all."**

The next day I had a chat with Bill, and told him "here I am... and I offer to go to wherever you say, **but would love to go back East... Detroit in particular."** This had come from what I had grown to feel... not only that the culture in California was rather superficial, but that we had really enjoyed the East... and, that I would enjoy another challenge of starting something from scratch. We had done that previously in Baltimore, in D.C. and virtually the same in San Jose. All had flourished... **was I more a pioneer than a settler?**

Bill told me "no, Chuck Reinhold is going to Detroit", so I began to look at other cities... Boston? Cleveland? Buffalo? (how dumb can I be... Cleveland? Buffalo?). But several weeks later Bill called and said: **"Chuck isn't going to Detroit, and we'd like for you to go there... let me know in two weeks."** Wow! Just what I had wanted.

I laid out five or six criteria, which would give confirmation that this is what God wanted us to do. In a very short time, most of the criteria were confirmed... though a little iffy on having my own kids say ok. When Sports Illustrated came one week, on the cover was a picture of the Detroit Piston's basketball coach. Without saying anything, I gave the magazine to Pete... and just looking at the cover, he quickly said: **"you're not going to convince me, dad."**

But what I felt most strongly about was that **my innards, my heart**, would need to feel a strong confirmation. **So how would I know that?** Then came one of those incredible moments that God provides on occasion. One evening… almost midnight… I was in the living room, kneeling at the sofa, praying, and said **"Lord, do you want us to stay here? or leave?… how will I know?"**

And there was a 'voice'… not audible, of course, but very clear… **"the Scriptures!"**

"Of course, Lord, but where?"

"Mark 10." I thought… hmmm… Mark 10, and my mind was blank.

"Where Lord?"

"Mark 10." Still blank… and then I was thinking 'how was Paul led?,' and was going through the book of Acts in my mind. Blank.

"Where, Lord?"

"Mark 10."

Blank… where were other places in the Gospels, or elsewhere, even the OT, where there was 'leading'? This went on for a bit, and again I said, **"Where, Lord?"**

"Mark 10!"… a little more emphatic this time. (Later on I concluded that the Holy Spirit had closed my mind, as I would naturally have thought of Mark 10:45, a key verse in Mark, and which I knew very well.)

"Where, Lord?… do you want us to stay or leave… how will I know?"

"Mark … 10!"

This was so strong… but still just not sure where this was going. So I said **out loud**, **"Mark 10?"…** and it was as if there was an echo… '**Mark teeennnnn'**

On an end table was a Catholic bible, and I opened it to Mark 10… never got past the first line…

"And after he left that place…"

"Thank you, Lord."

The next day I told Patti and the kids, and Pete said: "what'd you do then, dad?" I said "I cried," and he said: "I bet." (Did my kids see me as not being able to cry?… always strong?) But it couldn't have been more clear that we were to leave… **destination Detroit.**

I had only been to Detroit once, when one of my Seattle Pacific teammates needed to go to Michigan to pick up a new Pontiac for his dad. He suggested that 3 of us hitch-hike back there during spring break, wanting me to be the lead on this, since I had hitch-hiked a lot. I saw an ad in the Seattle paper "**drive my car to Denver**… you pay the gas, I pay the oil." We did this and saw why the ad… we used **35 quarts of oil to Denver** in this big Packard. From there we hitch-hiked to Pontiac … wild trip… each of us wearing our letter sweaters with a big '**S**' on the front, which of course was a great help in getting rides.

* * * * * * * * * * *

"And After He Left That Place"

So where do I start in a **Detroit move**? We had been planning on a 6-month sabbatical, beginning in the fall (1965), hoping to go to Switzerland to study (scholar Bud!). But now I figured that instead we would move to Detroit... take those 6 months to get acclimated... lay the groundwork for a YL ministry. I wrote to a number of Chambers of Commerce... got maps... did what I could to get data and information, and concluded we would move to **Birmingham**, an upper-middle-class northern suburb... and, developed a five-year plan.

The entire state of Michigan had only one YL staff person, located in Lansing. That summer while in Colorado I saw and met with him, to talk about the move to Detroit. We chatted a bit, and then he said to me **"have you ever thought of Ohio?"** Huh? What's this all about? It was obvious to me that he had qualms about my coming to Michigan. So I wrote his boss, the Great Lakes Regional Director (and who would become my boss) asking him "what would you suggest as to procedure for starting YL in Detroit" ... where virtually no one had even heard of YL. His response came back... "move there, get a job, start a YL club, and over time develop adult interest for support"... i.e., come in the back door. **What a hit to my gut...** exactly the **opposite** of how I would go about it... come in the **front** door. "Lord, what are you saying?"

That was a wrenching short period of time... **"do you want us to stay? or leave?"**... **"and after he left that place."** But I became convinced that I could not go to Detroit... operating not only at odds with those to whom I would be responsible, but contrary to my modus operandi. This was now 5 months later, and when I told the kids that we weren't going to Detroit, Pete said **"but dad, what about Mark 10?"**

I drove up to Berkeley to tell Bob Mitchell, my boss, that I wasn't going to Detroit, and why. After brief conversation he asked me how well I knew **Jake Coss**, the San Diego area director. I told him we had just had him speak at a week-end camp in San Jose, and that when I took him to the airport on Sunday he asked if I had ever thought of moving to **Southern California.** That was it… at least in Mitch's mind.

The So. Cal. scene in YL was bizarre… every staff person but one was in therapy, and the word around the country was that YL there was sliding into the ocean. Mitch said "we need someone there who can work with Jake, and to oversee the Fuller Seminary student leadership program… I know why you're not going to Detroit… **we want you to go to Southern California and be the Regional Director."** I told him "I **don't want to be a R. D.,** and I **don't want to live in So. Cal**. He said "pray about it… go be with the staff there for a day." I basically said 'no thanks,' but he leaned.

In December I flew down to be with the staff for a day, but what I was clearly thinking was… **no way am I coming down here**. The morning was a business session… then after lunch we had a session to talk of my thoughts and the Region. I took 10-15 minutes to share how I felt God had led in Patti's and my life through the years, and then asked if they had any questions.

"Are you going to change us?" Boom… strong, direct and candid… and I told them I didn't think it was our responsibility to change anyone. "You've heard all kinds of things about

Southern California… what are your thoughts." We had good, open interaction… and then a group of us had dinner together, after which I headed home… **couldn't wait to get out of there**. What a wild bunch.

I was seated by a window, and as the plane took off… and I'm rehearsing my speech to Mitch about **going east** somewhere… I looked down over the lights of **Los Angeles,** and the most **overwhelming feeling** came over me… "**that's home… these are my people**!" Again, it was almost like a voice, and exactly the **opposite** of anything I had thought of, or wanted… no way was I going there. And now this strong sense that this is where I was supposed to be… **this** was home… I'm not **going** home … **oh God, what are you saying?**

As we prayed about this, Patti and I both felt that **"after he left that place"** was what God had told us… it was **just south, not east.** So starting in January I began to commute from San Jose. I would have my Camden club on Monday night, fly to Burbank early on Tuesday, and come back late Thursday night… we would move in the summer.

The week before I began my **weekly commute to L.A.**, I had been in the beautiful home of a YL committee couple, who suggested that when I came down I could stay in their home… they would be at their beach home. It was high in the hills above Pasadena, with the entry through a back drive, since there were 30-40 steps up to the front from the street. "We'll leave the key under the mat."

The first Tuesday I flew down I stayed at the office until after midnight… lots of stuff to get caught up on, and no need to go to an empty house. When I arrived at the home there was no key under the mat. So I walked around to the other side of the house, and there the door had been left unlocked, and the light on in the spare bedroom... how very thoughtful... there was even a pair of pajamas on the bed for me. What hospitality!

I undressed, and standing there in just my shorts, a voice came... **"who's there?"**

"It's Bud"... obviously they didn't go away as they had said.

Then a woman poked her head around the corner, and with a face all plastered up and curlers in her hair, she screamed... **"what are you doing here?"**

"Isn't this the Entwhistles?"

"No... get out of my house!"

Wrong house... welcome to the zoo, Bud.

But the commute grew old fast, and we decided to move in March.

* * * * * * * * * *

Southern California

It was suggested that I **not** move to **Glendale,** as that was where the Regional Director had lived, and YL there was a mess. But I felt that I should be where strong leadership was needed at this time... and, with the Regional office in Glendale, we moved there... at least temporarily.

Of course moving in March meant having the kids change school and friends in the middle of the year, but they seemed game for it. One unusual hitch had to do with both Cherie and Pete. In San Jose she was a freshman in **high school**, but in Glendale the **9th grade** was in **junior hi**... so a demotion? For Pete... in San Jose he was in **junior high**, 7th grade. But he was much younger than most of the others in his class, and he was feeling it. So in moving to Glendale we had him go **back to the 6th grade**... and **elementary school**... which of course was fortuitous, as we would see later in his football years.

My initial task was to get the overall feel of the staff and region... and decide where we wanted to locate as a family. I ran across a map with the demographic breakdown of the whole L.A. basin **by income**... so one could see areas of wealth... e.g. Palos Verdes, Beverly Hills, etc.... and areas of very low income, e.g. Watts. I went to that map company and found a similar map, with the same breakdown by **average age in a family**. I superimposed the two, to see where families of ages similar to ours lived... and our income level... or a bit higher. The **Whittier/La Habra** area was just right... and, the YL staff person in that area had just left, so they also needed an Area Director, and I could serve also in that role.

The area was a good fit for us. We got our first dog, a German shepherd... trained her in 3 days to bring in the L.A. Times. Cherie became senior class secretary... and asked me to start a YL club in her school, La Habra Hi, which I did. Shy Phil was coaxed into going out for little league baseball (later, balls were signed and given to him for his feats... **"no hitter"** (pitching) ... **"grand slam home run"**... and more). And what fun we as a family had going to the beaches those summer days… Phil never wanted to come out of the water.

It didn't take long to discover the staff issues of which YL headquarters had been concerned, and for the first two years most of what I did was to resolve personnel problems. This was a group of very gifted people, but some mavericks, doing their own thing… appalling in some ways. Of the 12 student staff from Fuller Seminary, only 2 were leading YL clubs… a consequence of some of the turmoil in the Region, with no training or supervision. One Area Director, recognized nationally, was keeping two sets of books… another Area Director's committee and staff wanted him to quit… in San Diego Jake seemed to be struggling… and more.

I knew I had to meet with Jake. When we met, after some small talk I said to him: "I sense that Jake Coss is really struggling with some things," and he replied, "what did you say?" I simply repeated that, and he just broke down, began weeping. He shared a bit, and I suggested that we meet two weeks later. When we met I suggested that he take a year's leave of absence, then return with renewed spirit. He cussed me out… then six months later wrote me **"thanks for doing me the greatest favor in my life."**

There were other staff with problems, different in kind but similar in degree. One of the things I learned from those first years was that it was more important to do what was best for the person, more than for the organization… that if it was the best for the person, it was win/win.

* * * * * * * * * *

The **Watts riots** had occurred the summer of 1965, and a big part of that community had burned to the ground... the beginning of huge social unrest across the country in the mid and late sixties. I was thinking that perhaps we in YL should do something in that area, so I invited **George Sheffer**, YL's **national urban director**, to come out and help us ask the right questions. I was able to get the #2 man in the **L.A.P.D.** to show us the area, and began to realize how little I knew about the urban scene... and blacks in particular. So I decided to go **live in Harlem and Lower East side for a while**, to learn what I could from our YL staff there. What an education... in bed with **cockroaches,** climbing those urine-smelling stairs... saw **rats** in the windows of a meat market, from where we purchased our meat... but those weeks proved to be invaluable for me in years to come.

The ministry in Southern California was hard... but challenging, in the sense of creating a new vision and direction for the Region. There was a lot of nurturing necessary for young staff, and we were seeing good progress. Some good leaders and staff were beginning to come out of Fuller Seminary... and, we had some outstanding school teachers who were coming on staff.

Early in my third year there Bill Starr, YL President, asked me to consider moving to Chicago... to become the Regional Director in the **Great Lakes.** I told him I didn't think my work was finished where I was... and, why me? He said: **"you're a good manager, and we have the same problems there as we had here... we need you there."** I told him, as I had told Mitch earlier re Southern California... **"not interested."** He asked us to pray about it, and go back there for a visit (heard that before?). I'm not sure I prayed about it, as I had little interest in going there... but I did take a brief trip there, after which I told him... '**not interested.**' He came back with... "keep praying about it, and **take Patti for 4-5 days there.**" Yuk! But "ok."

We flew back there in early September, 1968, and it was one of those hot, humid weekends... I was sure that this was not for me... neither saw nor felt anything that was appealing... and my response to Bill was still "**not interested.**" He said: "**keep praying about it.**"

By nature I'm somewhat of a strategist, a tactician (I've come to believe that the **gift of Faith** is equated with **vision**... seeing what can be done, how to do it, and bring people around who will make it happen.) And I've always enjoyed a challenge... taking a calculated risk... in 4 careers I've usually not known what my compensation would be when I started... and, essentially have never had a pension... money would never determine what I would do. Also, I never knew what I was going to do next when I resigned, the first time at age 52.

I'm quite sure I wasn't praying about "**leaving that place,**" but one day a thought hit me... the greater Los Angeles area has **no cohesive factor**... no area relates naturally to any other, and it would be difficult to build a collective regional vision among staff and Committees. What I had seen in Chicago was **The Loop**... where **everything** in metropolitan Chicago **connects**... so different from L.A.

I called Bill Starr to say "**yes, I'll go... but next year, after our daughter graduates from high school**"... and Patti was just finishing her college degree. He agreed to that... but then in mid-December he said **"we can't wait... you've got to go now."** I didn't want to move the family again mid-year... so once again I began the commute. Starting in January I flew to Chicago for **10 days each month**... with the less-than-scintillating job of being Regional Director for both Southern California **and** the Great Lakes.

In retrospect, one of the things I learned about myself in L.A. was that I didn't need to see the end result of my work in order to be fulfilled. In building there for the future, that existing 'building' had to be **razed first**... unfun, ugly stuff... **then lay a foundation**. I felt that is what I had done... cleaned up an existing mess, then laid a solid foundation... and for whoever came to build the superstructure, there was solid ground. The new building may even look different from my design, but that's ok... it would stand. And it felt good.

I know that I didn't understand then what I would come to see later... the implications of being gone 10 days a month. With Patti taking 20 hours of college classes, and **four school-age children** at home... how incredibly unfair to all of them to have such an **absentee father.** They all seemed to do well, but there was no doubt a cost to this, however that might be viewed... both then and later.

We moved to **Chicago** in late August, and at the last minute were able to get Cherie accepted at Hope College, in Michigan. Less than one week after settling into our new home, she was off to college, and later on I would wonder if perhaps I had made a mistake... by not moving a year earlier, so she could make friends in her new community. Now, when she came 'home' for a week-end… a strange environment… no friends… a difficult transition. Later on I would conclude that a move 2 years before graduation would be more ideal… more time for friends and transition.

CHAPTER 5

GREAT LAKES REGION

Metro Chicago was being overseen by Bob, Area Director in the Near West, and living in **Hinsdale.** But he didn't really have a grasp on the urban culture… had become excessively rigid… and would not allow the urban staff to connect in any way with the suburban ministry, nor vice versa. Granted, and as I later discovered, some of the urban staff were a bit marginal in their faith, but they were doing some incredible things in the city.

We had some black staff who were very good in being in touch with what was going on in the streets, and following the recent murder of Malcolm X, they were helping to calm a very tense situation. Sadly, staff woman Joan Campbell's husband was killed while trying to quell a riot.

But **YL was at an impasse in the entire Chicago area**. In not really understanding black or urban culture… nor the ministry the staff was having there… Bob had driven a wedge between the urban and suburban staff… a most disquieting time for both groups… 0 communication.

So, like in moving to Glendale, I settled in the area most troubled, where Bob was living… it was just the right place for us. **Hinsdale** was the affluent community in the western suburbs, and contacts there would be of great value for the future… and, with great schools, it was so good for the 3 boys. All 3 played varsity sports, which also gave me great connections with parents… my weekly Young Life club averaged **over 100** for the 9 years I was there. **Pete** was All-State/All-American receiver in football his senior year… voted as one of the top 50 players in the country. **Phil** did well enough to get into Florida Institute of Technology, and **Steve** was an Illinois State Scholar his junior year.

Now with much more geography to cover in this new Region, I had to travel a good bit, needing to be with staff throughout the 4-state region… the first five years I averaged almost a flight a week out of O'Hare airport. And I had to work through some of the same issues with staff as in So. Cal.

I was gone too much from home those first few years, but we were seeing some great things happening. The year I arrived there were **11** staff in the entire 4-state region… 3 years later only 3 of those were still with us, but we now had **33 on staff**. There was a tremendous spirit among staff, and I had initiated ministry in several new cities, especially in Michigan… Flint, Grand Rapids, Kalamazoo, Muskegon… (Michigan… yes, **Detroit… "No"**)… and also in Anderson, Indiana … Peoria, Illinois… and Madison, Wisconsin. The latter start was most intriguing.

One day I received a phone call from a lady in Madison. She was interested in getting a ministry going with teenagers there, and had inquired into everything she could imagine. She kept being told about this **'Young Life'**, but could find nothing about it. One evening she went to the public library to see if there was anything she could find there… to no avail. As she was leaving, she saw this gentleman studying at a table, and for some reason felt compelled to ask him… "Sir, I'm sorry to bother you, but I'm trying to get information about a youth organization, called Young Life… would you happen to know anything about them?" Whereupon **Bill Starr, President of Young Life**, looked up, and said: "yes, I think I know a bit about them"… he happened to be in Madison for a special series. Doesn't God have fun orchestrating unusual circumstances!

* * * * * * * * * *

I had decided that I wanted to participate in all the areas of ministry each of the Area Directors had, so I assumed the role of Area Director for the Near West, and had my own club and Committee. One of the things I wanted to do was to immerse suburban folk in the city… get them involved in some way. **Bill Busch** had several kids in YL, was Catholic, owned his own business, and a most outgoing person. On one occasion he said to me **"Bud, this Young Life is such a hell of a good thing… damn it all, what can we do to help?"** Gulp! I said: "let me think about it." A few weeks later he came back with the same message… I think verbatim… so I set up a meeting with **7 couples**, most of them like Bill and Nancy Busch. We discussed a dozen things they might do… and then, in a rather bold move, I invited all 7 couples on the Committee. So would they fit in?

My primary goal for our next Near West Committee meeting was to begin bridge-building with YL's urban ministry in the city. About **$3500** had been contributed the previous year from individuals in our area to YL urban, and the next month our Near West budget committee would be presenting the budget for the next year. I wanted to get more funds raised for urban... what would be a strategic way we might do that? So I intentionally invited our urban staff to come to this next Committee meeting, and they shared what God was doing in the city... the needs, etc... knocked the socks off this crowded room, the normal dozen plus 7 new couples.

At the end of the meeting our Committee chairman asked if I would close in prayer, and I said: "yes, but after several of you pray." There were a couple of nice, generic prayers, and then **Bill Busch,** sitting on the floor to my right, came out with... and I can still hear his gruff voice... **"Lord, you know I'm not used to this, but I think I'm beginning to discover what you want me to do, and I ask you to give me the courage to do it... amen."** Out came the handkerchiefs, and that was the beginning of an incredible journey for Bill... and the Committee. The next month when our budget committee met, the decision was to send a tithe of our Area's income for YL urban ministry... and that next year Near West people contributed **more than $30,000.** And, 30 years later Bill is still attending a weekly breakfast-Bible study I had started for dads of club kids.

* * * * * * * * * * **

Chicago Pot-Pourri

My first year in Chicago I got a call from **Keith Swagerty,** who had been in the first club I had in San Jose... Camden Hi. He was playing professional basketball, knew he was going to be traded, and decided he had had enough... so called and asked if I could use him. We developed several ideas, and he joined me on staff... from the highest salary on his pro team, to $500 a month. I had rented office space in the **Loop**, right on the corner of Michigan and Madison... we were going to really connect with corporate Chicago (dreamer!) But on occasion that spring Keith and I would say to Jane, my secretary... "we have a long luncheon, be back around 4"... and then we'd jump on the El and go to **Wrigley Field for a Cubs game**.

The main thing Keith did was to set up YL's first overseas basketball trip... to **Australia,** where he had contacts. We took 8 high school seniors, and had a week of assemblies in schools in Brisbane... played the local school's team (killed them all)... then had 2 week-end camps, each with about **70** kids. I was the speaker, and noting that the culture was so incredibly conservative, I presumed it was from a strong religious context. So I figured I could skip the normal first night **introductory talk**, and get right into it. **Wrong!** I've never felt such **0 feedback** in my life... I felt as if I was speaking to a wall.

Afterwards I talked to one of the local counselors, and she said their **understanding of the Gospel was about 0.** So I backed up for the Sat. morning and evening talks... back to the basics... then saw one of the most amazing responses I've ever seen at a camp. We had set up tables for a sort of coffee-house flavor after the Saturday evening talk... would have a basketball player at each table, to interact with the kids. That evening kids were **still around the tables at 1 a.m.**... .and... two years later there were 25 of them still meeting weekly for Bible study. We followed those 2 weeks with a week in **New Zealand,** with the same kind of results. The trip set the stage for starting YL in Australia, with a staff man moving there a couple of years later

* * * * * * * * * *

I have always wanted to think **Kingdom** more than institution, and felt that we could utilize the contacts we have via Young Life for more than just a teen ministry. Hal Edwards was a minister friend from Los Angeles who moved to Chicago at the same time as we, and was heading up a ministry of small groups in metro-Chicago for **key lay people.** I asked him to have lunch one day... we met in a small restaurant down in the Stock Yards, and I threw out an idea... told him he'd get all the credit, since he had good contacts with Christian leaders in the area. What if a group of these began to meet together on a regular basis... "a support group... **a think tank for what God might want to do in Chicago?"**

A group of us began meeting, and in discussing how our mutual responsibilities might interconnect, I suggested that **we go to Pittsburgh,** to see what was going on there... the **Pittsburgh Offensive**.

So 4 of us went to Pittsburgh for 3 days, to see the incredible thing that God was doing in carrying out the vision of the venerable **Sam Shoemaker**, who one day stood high on the hill across from Pittsburgh's Golden Triangle, and prayed that **"the day would come when Pittsburgh would be as known for God as it is for steel."** (In my opinion, that city has had more spiritual vitality among business leaders than any city I know of... Reid Carpenter and a committed core group have been carrying on Sam's vision via a life-long commitment to a city... a **'Theology of Place'.**)

Our group, now 8 or 10 of us, began to meet monthly for an entire day, to be of **support to one another**, and then to '**dream Chicago.**' We would spend the morning hours listening to each other, sharing joys and struggles... praying for each in our respective work/ministry... and then spend the afternoon in strategy for the city. This commitment to each other became a top priority for each of us, and years later I was invited back as **Founder** to celebrate the 25th anniversary of the **Chicago Network...** with the meeting in the office of the President of Chicago State University. Numerous non-profits were formed as a result of the collective efforts of the group... impacting Chicago.

* * * * * * * * * *

One of the men in the Chicago Network was **Bruce Bickel**, Midwest Director for Fellowship of Christian Athletes... a great athlete himself, backup to the great All-pro football player Roger Staubach. One day I suggested that we play racquetball, which we did. A few days later when I was with one of his staff, Roger, we talked about Bruce... his athleticism... and I casually mentioned that I had beat him in a game of racquetball. Roger couldn't believe it... "**no one beats Bruce**". I told him it was very close... 21-18... and that Bruce had said maybe we could play again someday, which we did. That second game I'll never forget... suddenly, I almost never saw the ball... it was mostly just a blur... whoooooshhh!... **10-0 score**, and I couldn't figure out what was happening. But then I noticed... **now** he was playing with his **right hand.** Before he had never said a word.

* * * * * * * * * *

People like **Bill Leslie** and **Ray Bakke** joined us in the Network… two of the most prominent men nationally in urban ministry, and certainly the two most influential as mentors for me in urban matters. Bill and I became 'soul mates'… the closest friend I've ever had. He was minister of **LaSalle Street Church**… a church of **300** and a **budget of $5 million… literally**. He had developed numerous non-profits… for housing (an $11 million project in the heart of Cabrini-Green, on a total investment of $1000 from each of 5 area churches), for seniors, counseling, justice, etc.

We began to attend LaSalle Street Church… 20+ miles from Hinsdale to central city Chicago, but Bill was both a good preacher and a genuine visionary… it was so good to be a part of that body. The first Sunday we drove down I parked on the street behind the church. After the service we got in the car… I turned the key… **nothing.** My battery was stolen… welcome to the city, Bud.

One day Bill asked Patti to pray about starting a tutoring program for kids at Wells High School, right next to **Cabrini-Green,** Chicago's biggest housing project… **85% on welfare** and where 6 policemen were killed one year. Patti prayed, and said **"Lord, if you want me to do this, you have to remove all fear."** She recruited 25 teachers, and they began in a **warehouse** in Cabrini. There were times she would be **all alone there, at night…** numerous blacks around, but she was **never afraid**. The program grew… was later named **Cycle,** and came to have a million dollar budget. One of her first students, **Alvin Bibbs**, is now on the staff of **Willow Creek Church.**

* * * * * * * * * * *

During our years in Chicago Patti and I were part of a couple of 'small groups'... fellowship type groups meeting monthly. One I named the **harmless group**... nothing ever happened... the other the **wine and cheese group**, a fun 4 couples. One of the men in the former group was chief fireman for the **Indy 500 race**, and he invited me to be on the fire crew for one of those Memorial Day races. The first year I took Pete with me, and the second year took Steve. There we were, **right in the pits with the racing cars**. During the race, when a car would pull into the pit for a fuel stop or a tire change, we had to stand there, with one foot on the railing and a fire hose in hand... fortunately, they were never needed. But I can still hear the **incredible roar** when the announcer said over the loudspeaker, "**Gentlemen, start your engines,**" and 33 high-powered race cars all started at once... **VAARRUUMMPPHH!!** What a fun experience... **inside the Indy 500!**

* * * * * * * * * * *

One enjoyable diversion for me during my latter years in Chicago... but I allude to it here although the occasion occurred years later in Seattle, at the annual County Leadership Breakfast. **Jeff Kemp** called me over and said "Bud, I want you to meet **George Karl**" (coach of the **Seattle Sonics** at that time.) We exchanged greetings and then I said: "we have one thing in common, George... **I used to be with the Chicago Bulls.**" Having played pro basketball, he knew the players, and said to me "what's your name again?" I told him. "And you were with the Bulls?"... his curiosity piqued. I said yes, and he asked me when, and I told him in the 70's, and then said "you know... Chet Walker, Bob Love, Tom Boerwinkle... "and named others... so he knew what I was talking about.

"What's your name again?"... he was really perplexed, and I told him my name again. "And you were with the Bulls?" Then I said: "yes, I was **Benny the Bull**" (the Bull's mascot). Great chuckle. But those were some fun times... being in the locker room with the players, getting dressed in that red flannel uniform, with the huge head of a bull. At each game, after the players were announced, then over the loudspeaker came "**and now, the greatest Bull of them all... heeeeeere's Benny**! And I would go running out onto the court, cavorting up and down in front of both benches. But what fun, filling in occasionally for a friend as Benny the Bull.

* * * * * * * * * * *

Grace... God's Generosity

We had grown almost exponentially, so I decided to split the Region into 3... handing off Michigan and Indiana as one Region, and Illinois, Wisconsin and Iowa as another. We had 8 separate Areas now just in metro-Chicago, and I wanted to focus on the urban-suburban interrelatedness.

The annual budget for all Regional Directors was primarily made up from an assessment charged to each Area budget in the Region... but in most cases the R.D. had to raise extra funds. I had to raise about $15,000 a year to make up the difference, but I never felt that to be a problem... even though now with less Areas... less income. The new fiscal year would begin in October, and in mid-September, while I was praying the thought came to me that I wanted to have a relationship with donors that was not connected with asking them for $, that I would just ask God to provide what I needed.

So I said "**Lord, I'm not going to ask a single person for funds this year... I'm going to trust you for that.**" It felt right, and I never gave another thought to my financial needs.

In December Lisa, a former club gal then at the University of Chicago, came over to the house and asked if any funds were needed for YL... I said: "try me." She said her dad was selling a business, and might be interested in donating something to YL... maybe around **$10,000.** So I told her of my need, and prayer... but then heard nothing more from her. In February her mother called and asked where to send some money for YL. I told her it should be sent to Colorado, but that it could be credited locally. She said **"ok, it's $100,000."** When I picked myself up off the floor, I thought, "Lord, you're just too amazing."

Although I could designate the funds wherever I chose, I had the fun of sitting with the family, asking where they would like to see it go. Lisa had become very involved with urban YL, so we set aside one-third for that... some for the Area budget... some for a classmate of Lisa who was going on YL staff the next year... and some for my regional budget.

The sequel to this came a month later, when I received a phone call one afternoon... "Bud, did you know that **Jane** is in the hospital, and may not live through the night?" Jane was very close to Lisa's mother, and when I went to the hospital late that evening, Jane was in isolation... a glass-enclosed room...

meningitis and encephalitis. Covering me from foot to head, the nurse took me in to see her, and I asked if Jane could hear me… the nurse said "no."

I took Jane's hand, and said: "**Jane, this is Bud.** A few years ago I was lying right where you are, with the same illness. God was gracious to me, and I'm going to ask Him to be gracious to you." I prayed briefly, and was there for only 3 or 4 minutes.

The next morning I was in the shower, and while thinking of Jane a thought came to me… and I prayed, out loud: "**Lord, would you take the generosity of giving by the Tieszens, and translate that into your generosity of healing for Jane**"… and what felt like a huge electric shock went through me. I said aloud: "thank you, Lord." (We know that real prayer often originates from God… I'm sure those were **His thoughts,** not mine.) Two weeks later Jane was back in the classroom, and I had the fun of sharing with Lisa's parents perhaps the residual effect of their generosity.

And Lisa… from this affluent home… graduated from the University of Chicago the next year, then went to San Francisco to work with the Mennonites… for **$25 a month** and room and board… a heart for the urban under-class.

CHAPTER 6

THE TIPPING POINT

Or... a mid-life crisis? Most of us can look back on our lives and see that a given event or decision influenced us deeply in some way, or moved us in a direction different from where we were going. Our getting involved with Young Life had totally changed where we were originally heading.

It was some time in the early or mid-70's when one night **Patti** sat up in bed... and said: **"Bud, you have one week to decide if you want us to stay married."** Clunk!! Even as I write this, I feel that heavy weight that suddenly came upon me... what in the world brought this on... total surprise.

For all these years Patti had been such a support to me... good mother... solid in her faith... and now suddenly, out of the blue... this? Of course, as I learned later, we men can be blind to what our wives are **feeling,** let alone thinking... caught up in our busywork. By nature I had a strong work ethic, and got things done, but was so unaware of **not being in touch with my feelings**... and as a result, certainly not in touch with hers.

In those years of approaching the 'empty nest' syndrome, Patti had begun to take graduate courses at a seminary nearby, primarily under Dr. David Augsburger, an incredible professor and author. The classes on **Marital and Family Therapy** and **Conflict Management** were putting her in touch with her 'self' in totally new ways... seeing that her identity had really been as an extension of me... being a faithful and supporting wife to a person in ministry. But who was **she,** really? And my controlling nature made it easy for me to take advantage of that... not really knowing what I was doing to her.

As happens in those kinds of courses, one does a great deal of self-analyses, discovering one's own person. Elizabeth O'Connor, in her book **Journey Inward, Journey Outward,** says: **"we are the absentee landlords of our own selves,"** and no doubt that was true of both Patti and me. But I could hide that in my work. It was about that same time that I was sort of dragging, so one of our friends in Hinsdale set up an appointment for me at the Holistic Clinic. After taking the stress test, the doc said: "You have no stress... **how many hours a week do you work?**" I said "about **70.**" He said "no more than **55**"... and I began to feel much better. **A workaholic???** Intimacy avoidance?

What I began to realize was that I wasn't even close to being in touch with my feelings. At one point Patti said to me **"get out of your head, and come to your senses."** So during that week I agreed to go together for counseling... and not knowing where to go with all this, I decided to take those same courses she had taken. What a mind-opener, as I began to see how right she was... not only that I wasn't connecting with her at all, but I wasn't connecting with my own self. **I rarely used feeling words**... didn't delineate the difference of **feeling vs thinking.**

About this time I was at a Regional Director conference in Colorado, and there was considerable discussion on the role of women on staff. From one marginal comment I asked one of the women there, "how do you **feel** about that", (I was practicing what I was learning) and she said, "I feel that we **ought to**... "... not a response of **feeling**, but of **thinking.** Like many, I had usually **felt** in my head.

One part of the family therapy course was a study on **family systems**... including doing one's own, and I began the journey of interviewing every living member of my extended family... mother, siblings, aunts/uncles... ultimately a rather lengthy treatise. I was able to do it in a way that allowed for pretty candid openness... just "wanting to know more about how things were when I was growing up." Wow, what a revelation. In asking the question "who was strong and who wasn't", one sibling said: **"I don't connect weakness with our family!"...** perhaps a rather typical sense of denial, not really being honest with ourselves... "absentee landlords of our own selves." (Going through this process was not only helpful to me in walking through my own growth at that time, and a better understanding of myself, but for later on in doing a lot of pre-marital counseling.)

The next several years were very difficult for me... I was not only walking through a learning curve vocationally, but now a crisis in my marriage. Perhaps precipitating much of the latter were extreme societal changes, probably the worst of any decade in that century. The late sixties saw **riots** in our urban centers... intense **racial issues on integration** (Selma march, etc.)... the **'hippie' movement**... the **counter-culture... Viet Nam**... and not the least of which was the rise of the **feminist movement** at that time. No doubt an issue for Patti at this time was in seeing that she, as a woman, needed to have her own life… be her own person.

Our daughter, Cherie, had transferred to Grand Valley State her second year, and then dropped out after the first quarter. She ended up in a 'commune' in upstate New York… life for her took a different turn. Before long she ended up somewhere in Arizona, and we didn't see her for 3 years… didn't even know where she was. (I had wrestled through our alienation, and through a book on the **Prodigal Son** ultimately saw so clearly the need for **acceptance, without approval**… a great lesson for me.) One day there was a knock on the door, and there she stood, with this man in a long army trench coat, hair down to the middle of his back… **"hi, I'm John, and Cherie and I live together."** We invited them in, and after a week, John said, "you're the first Christians I've ever met that I liked." (He was Jewish.) Thank you Lord, I think I'm making progress.

So for me, I was going through the struggle of how to relate to and connect with the two most important women in my life. At one point as I journaled, I wrote about a line in one of the Beatles' songs, **"you'll let me love you honey, but why, why can't I touch you?"**… i.e., we can make love, but the real us never touches. That was me… not really touching or connecting with Patti on an intimate level, a level of feeling with her in her world. I wrote what most of us know… that perhaps the greatest gift a parent can give to their child is to love their spouse… and I didn't have the slightest idea how to do that… at least not in depth.

At times I felt discouraged… just wanted to get on with life, and forget all this 'feely feely' stuff… but I knew she was right, and what I was learning under Augsburger was beginning to take root. I was making progress. Some years later I was taking a class on teaching the **Myers-Briggs** profile, and I showed as **ENFJ**. I asked the teacher if one's profile changed through life, and she said normally never... **unless** one has gone through a major crisis or life-change. That **F**, for '**Feeling**', was intriguing, since its counterpart is **T**, for '**Thinking**'... had I really made that change? Granted, it was about a 52/48 ratio... but... I was on a growing journey.

CHAPTER 7

A SABBATICAL

In YL we were allowed a **six-month sabbatical** every 7 years. I had planned on one in 1965, but the 'Detroit move' had precluded that. So since I was getting over my workaholism, I decided I would take the first three months off in 1976... (certainly would be over-doing it to take **six** whole months). I had been intrigued with the concept of **'community'**... and the role that plays in Christian growth. In a Fuller course, Dr. Roberta Hestenes had made the comment **"without community, faith limps ... it doesn't run."** So I decided to read up on that area, and then to go visit several Christian communities around the country.

I had already been to **Reba Place,** in Evanston, a large and joyous community where there is full sharing of all things in common... and read the Jackson's book *Living Together In A World Falling Apart.* I learned of a number of others around the country, and decided to visit **Church Of The Savior** (CoS) in Washington, D.C... **Church of the Redeemer** in Houston, an Episcopal charismatic church... and **Peninsula Bible Church** in Palo Alto, founded and led by Ray Stedman, author of *Body Life*. I read a number of books on community, and was most impressed with the writings of **Elizabeth O'Connor**, whose books were an expression of the life of CoS.

The following excerpts are from my **journal** during that time:

1-23 office for ½ hr.— noon, read and file work— evening to dinner w/ Wendell & Helen— good time— then home & the 4 of us talked about **how do we let the other know we love them** *1-25 slept in—relaxed—finished Cosby's book—challenged! especially pp151-3—why am I so satisfied (though not really) with a* **mediocre "life"** *– the life had w/out death. The pain of death is repugnant – I so want & need approval of* men *– O God, how can I become totally satisfied w/ your approval alone — Oh the pain of self-absorption – Ugh! Academically aware of God's rule in my life - but not experiencing the freedom, joy, peace…* **oh for that peace!**

*1-26 read a bit (***Body Life***) I can't get away from the whole idea of the Christian life style being that which embraces the hurt and pain of the poor & oppressed – everywhere. What does that mean to me? I don't know, which is a bit frustrating — I want to* do something! *Is God readying me for some task, or is it simply His needing to make me more just His man? I can't really sort out whether I just need to be needed, or for purely God's & people's sake want to be at that point where I can most help eliminate hurt & pain — oh that men would know of God's love & beauty! — especially those who need it most.*

1-28 played racquetball w/ John Block—swam—then bank & misc. errands—pack for trip & to airport 5 p.m.— flight to Pitt, then to D.C. John Hartsock picked me up & we talked till after 1 a.m.

*Mon.2-2 left for appt w/ Betty O'Connor—absolutely fascinating 2 hrs. After an hour she called Gordon Cosby in—I asked the question "what role does the community play in ascertaining gifts?" — whereupon Betty & Gordon engaged in a ½ hr dialogue on this subject—Gordon was saying the community is imperative, that one's gifts are confirmed as others confirm & validate thru response. Betty was saying that her new thinking on this was that the **gifts aren't perhaps as important as one's "call"—what is one supposed to <u>do</u>**—and his **gifts will help him fulfill the call**—& usually others will confirm the call via positive response —but on occasion one may have a valid call but the group doesn't respond— the person may be creatively ahead of the group.*

Many heavy thoughts as I try to personalize this—do I really want to pay the price for such a commitment? I sense such a rightness to their commitments, & such a shallow life at our church—more commitment to an evangelical creed than to a living person. And I guess that's so much me too. Read last night in Nehemiah—greatly challenged (bothered) by 9:36—"Slaves among all this abundance" Wow! How enslaved I am to myself amid all God's Grace! The pharaoh in me holds me from being released.

How can I capture the last week? What does it all mean? I believe I've experienced a bit of the book of Acts, where believers cared & shared & gave their lives away in joyous fellowship—the CoS people have no concern about making the church function—all their time and energies are spent in <u>being</u> the Church —being with each other in deep and meaningful ways —how do I integrate this?

*2-8 slept in—read paper—then **Journey Inward/Journey Outward** —being challenged in several areas — unbelievable how we –I feel the middle-class comforts are valid & necessary,*

*& so will do anything to maintain such. The person free enough to live w/out such in a life of real "**giving**" must be really free—I feel an occasional glimpse of what that must mean—to have <u>life</u> as a vocation—my awareness of self & possessions keeps me so much from enjoying w/ abandon the present. I need to learn what it means to be silent before God & to listen to his voice—can I recognize it? (the Olympic speed skater who was asked if she could hear her coach's voice over the yelling crowds— "of course, **I have come to recognize his voice because we are together so much – I'd recognize it anywhere**")*

CHAPTER 8

PORTLAND

Patti had never seen her father... when she was born, he left her and her mother in San Francisco, and returned to Cuba (see **Cuba** in chapter 18). I knew of the gnawing question in her mind through the years... "**was I really not wanted?... what was he like?**"... there was something missing on her insides. So without telling her, in the evenings I would make phone calls... to every county and major city in Florida, asking for a **Demetrio Carvajal**. (That was before there were charges for an 'information' call.) I did this for several months, with the response???... **0.** Then I contacted former YL colleague Tom Getman, Mark Hatfield's chief aide, and he asked Mark to pursue the search, which he did via Social Security. Response? **"There is not a Demetrio Carvajal in the United States."** Then I told Patti what I had done, and although it was helpful information, those questions inside her remained.

Patti had only one full relative still living: an elderly Aunt in **Palo Alto,** a step-grandmother in **San Francisco,** a half-sister in **San Jose,** and a half-brother and half-sister in **Oklahoma.** But she was closest to the three in California, and I sensed a real desire on her part to be nearer to them. So at one point I said to her... **"you're more important to me than anything else, let's move west."** She was most responsive to the idea... so at a conference of Regional Directors I asked the Northwest Director if he had a spot out there for us. He was eager for us to come, and would carve out a new Region: **Oregon and Southwest Washington.** I went from having had the largest Region in the country to the smallest, and loved it.

In April of 1978 we went to **Portland** for a weekend, to meet with the YL Committee, and for them to meet us... to see if this would be a good fit. Everything clicked for all concerned... it was all systems 'go'. So I said to Patti, **"instead of going home on Monday, let's look at houses... we'll buy by Wednesday, and go home on Thursday."** (Oh, really?) We didn't even know where in the greater Portland area we would want to live... dreaming again? I wanted to be in the area of a key high school... always felt I wanted to provide a 'model' YL club, and decided on the area of Wilson Hi... and the **West Hills.** So I suggested to Patti that she head on home... I'd look for a house... **buy on Thursday... and come home on Friday.**

I got a realtor's multiple listing book, and saw only a few houses listed in the area of choice... drove by them, and selected three for a realtor to show me on Wednesday. Early that morning I was reading from **Mark 10**, in my Phillips N.T., and in the middle of the chapter James and John asked a question of Jesus... and he says to them: **"what do you want me to do for you?"** (It was to have each sit on either side of Jesus in his glory... not good.) Later on in the same chapter, a blind man calls out to Jesus for help, and Jesus says **"what do you want me to do for you?"** (good)... but it seemed interesting to me that those **same words**

from Jesus… on two different occasions… were on the **exact same line… on the opposite page.**

As I was taking a shower, suddenly there was this 'voice'… **"what do you want me to do for you?"** I couldn't believe it, but I said: **"Lord, help me buy a home today,"** and it felt like I heard **"ok."**

I went with the realtor to look at the three homes… none fit. But when I drove away from the last one, at the end of the block there was an **'Open House'** sign… it wasn't there the day before. I drove up that street, which narrowed into a 'lane', and I winded up a one-lane, two-way street… there was this Open House. **I liked it**, and asked what price they had on it. The realtor said the house wasn't for sale… this was **only for realtors**… that they would set a price at the end of the day. I asked "what time?"… "4:30." So I said, **"I'll be back at 4:30"**, which I was. We talked price, but she was firm on the asking price, since it wasn't even on the market yet. So I said **"I'll buy it"** … signed the papers for the purchase… and she told me to call her back at 7:00 p.m…. she'd do the paper work.

I went to dinner with a couple, **to celebrate**, and from the restaurant called her at 7. She said, "well, I have **2 offers**, so you'll have to call me back at 10:00 p.m." My heart sank… I was flabbergasted… **"what do you want me to do for you?"**… give me a heart attack? ("Oh ye of little faith"). I asked her if the other party had offered more, and she wouldn't say. So when I called her at 10, she asked if we could change the proposed closing date to two weeks later, and I said "yes." Then she said, **"it's yours!"**

Later on she told me what had happened... that the other party had written a deposit check for $3500... I had written one for **$5000...** and the seller said "I think they want it more," so chose us. But the **amazing** part was... the other party would **pay cash...** he was **a doctor... living nearby**... and we were coming from **out of town,** and would need to be **applying for a loan.** It just seemed to make no sense, humanly speaking. And, interestingly, the realtor told me that **the Open House sign wasn't supposed to be there,** but a block farther up the hill, where I would never have seen it, as I would have turned left, down the hill. Here again it seemed that God was doing something out of the ordinary for us... and **on Friday I flew home.**

(As I write this, I have just been reading through the Gospel of Mark, and last night was **Mark 10.** We recently bought a new home, **but our other isn't sold yet...** in the worst real estate market in decades. Tonight I read Mark 11... "I tell you, whatever you ask for in prayer, believe that you have received it, and it will be yours." Do I/we have enough faith to believe that?)

By now our 4 kids were out of the nest... **Cherie** was in Arizona... **Pete** had graduated from Wheaton College and was teaching in Korea... **Phil** was at Florida Institute of Technology... and **Steve** had gone to the University of Illinois. So even though we had thoroughly enjoyed our 9 years in Chicago, we felt a westward move was right at this time.

* * * * * * * * * *

The Agony

Most of YL in the Region was in metro-Portland… but also in Salem, Eugene and Vancouver, WA. That Fall I went to **Bend,** in central Oregon, to meet with a group who wanted to get YL started there. The next morning I left Bend about 6:00 a.m., on my way to meet with the regional staff in Eugene for an all-day conference. Doing 65-70 on a straight, 2-lane hi-way, I started to pass a truck… when suddenly I found myself **skidding… sideways**. I had hit **'black ice'…** (never heard of it, and you can't see it… in Chicago one can at least **see** the ice). Then suddenly everything was a **total blur**… and flying off the highway, I slammed into a big tree about 5 feet off the side of the road. (Years later, in going by there, glass was still imbedded in the tree.) When Patti got a call that morning from a hospital in Bend… **"we have Norman here,"** she knew something had gone wrong**… "Norman?"**

It was a virtual miracle that I lived… deep **concussion, 10 broken bones in my back**, broken pelvis. But the amazing thing was the **out-of-body** experience I had. At the point of contact with the tree, I found myself **spiraling rapidly upward**, at an angle, through a black tunnel… saying to Patti **"I'm going to beat you home, hon… hurry up"**… I knew I was going home to be with the Lord… but then woke up in the hospital. Later on I contacted the State Patrol and got the name of the truck driver who had stopped down the road… to say thanks, and to learn of what happened.

He told me that he knew when I started to pass him that I wouldn't make it… it took him half a mile to stop, and when he got out of his truck he couldn't walk on the highway… **too slippery**. He said I was lying on the ground, outside the car, with my right leg inside... no seat belt. But it was fortunate that Bend was the nearest hospital... being a major ski area, they had outstanding orthopedics. After a week in Bend, they flew me back to Portland in an air ambulance... **ouch... ouch...** every move during the transfer was **bad owie**, and I was quite immobile for more than a month

Suddenly, in late December Patti became very ill with **epiglottitis.** She couldn't swallow, and amid a Portland **ice storm,** when I called for a taxi, they couldn't come up our hill... roads too icy. So with my crutches, we got in the car, and rather miraculously got to the hospital. She was gasping for every breath, and when we arrived they performed an immediate tracheotomy.

Everything was ok for a day, but suddenly the situation became very serious. As we learned later, **in ICU she had contracted 3 separate viruses** through tubes placed in her neck for her to breathe. The viruses had caused 'matter' to begin encrusting around her lungs, which then began to collapse. They tried various drugs, but to no avail, so their only option was to **insert a tube through her side, with no anesthetic...** they wouldn't allow me near, but I heard the screams from down the hall.

The next day the doctor called, and told me to come quickly... that on at least a couple occasions she was within one breath of her last... it wasn't going well. I took The Living Bible translation with me, and read to her from Isaiah 43, inserting her name for others at certain places... "But now the Lord who created you, **Patti,** says **'Don't be afraid,** for I have ransomed you**; I have called you by name, you are mine.** When you go through deep waters and great trouble, **I will be with you.** When you go through rivers of difficulty, **you will not drown!**

Patti, others died that you might live: **you are precious to me and honored, and I love you."**

Through tears I prayed with her, and almost felt as though I was pronouncing last rites, as I saw her fade in and out of consciousness. But God was gracious, and she gradually improved... although ending up with life-long lung difficulties.

So there we were, a couple of invalids, in a new city... trying to care for each other. Steve thoughtfully left what he was doing in Illinois, and moved out to take care of us. I was able to resume my YL work after several months, although I still couldn't bend over... so when sitting, I had to gently lower myself into a chair. After Steve was there for a couple of months, he said to me one day; **"Dad, I know what I'm going to do for the next 7 years**... go to the U. of Oregon, then med school." (Although he wasn't able to get in med school right away, he persisted, and 3 years later was accepted.)

* * * * * * * * * *

The Ecstasy

One Sunday about 6 months after my accident, **communion** was being served at our church. We had co-pastors, both good friends, and one was up front to distribute the elements, with the other over on the side, to pray for anyone who so desired. But first, they had a doctor come and share about a virtual miracle he had experienced from one of his patients... a cure which had made no medical sense. Then, for some reason, my mind went to Bill Stenberg, who was on my staff in Chicago... a big 6'7" basketball player from Indiana U., and on one occasion he had asked if I would **baptize** him. I asked him why he wanted to be baptized, and he said: "because the Bible says so… and… **my ego needs it."**

That latter thought was what went through my mind as I sat there, sitting on my inner tube… do I want to walk up there and ask for prayer? That is usually a rather humbling act… but then, as the pastor held up the bread, and quoted from Scripture**… "this is my body, broken for you**… I thought … as the bread was being distributed… '**wouldn't it be great if Jesus' broken body were to touch my broken body.'**

So I rose from my chair and went up front… waiting for a couple of others ahead of me. Then Randy turned to me and said: "Bud, what do you want prayer for?" I told him **"you know, Randy, that I don't take a step without pain**… and I really don't know whether I fear more being healed, or not being healed." I'm not sure why I said that, but he took some oil and made the sign of the Cross on my right wrist … then prayed briefly… and I went back to sit down… gently.

After being home about two hours, I went out to the car to get something… dropped it on the ground, and then stooped over to pick it up**… yes… stooped over to pick it up**. I just started laughing, and kept **bending up and down**, **up and down**… and laughing. It was the first time I had been able to bend over for 6 months, and **I was perfectly well**. Well, almost… even from that time, there has been a small lump in my lower back, which leaves no pain… but I've often thought… did God leave that there as a forever reminder to me of His gracious love, and healing for me… maybe similar to Jacob's limp after he had wrestled with God… an always present reminder of a great God.

CHAPTER 9

SHORT-TERM MISSION

We enjoyed being in Portland very much... good friends... a home with a great view... and we were growing rapidly early on in this new Region. We had developed YL in several new areas and added a number of new staff... things were going well.

I began some long-range planning, including dividing up metro-Portland into several areas, and developing a leadership training program that looked like a winner. This included a **'20/20 Vision Corps'**... in which **college graduates would come on staff**... work 20 hours a week, and do 20 hours of ministry. We would consider them full staff, and begin new areas in this way, so that budgets wouldn't be so big from the start. There was strong interest in this right from the beginning, and we already had new clubs and Committees in **Bend** and **Coos Bay**.

Early that second year my boss came into town for an evaluation. I always liked to have at least a couple of my Area Directors be a part of any evaluation, as I felt more **accountability downward** than upward, since my boss was usually some distance away, and those working closely with me would have better perspective. It was a very positive session… all systems full speed ahead.

A couple of months later at our Divisional Conference, my boss, Bob (not his real name), grabbed me for lunch. In a manner that at best I would say was rather tactless, he suggested that I should probably leave YL. **Out of the blue!** He said that one of my staff had expressed to him concern about my lack of pastoral care… leadership in general… and that I hadn't given him adequate personal attention… (but who had even been a part of the affirming evaluation 2 months earlier, so I was rather taken aback by this.) I had expressed to Patti some months earlier my concern re him, that he may not make it as an Area Director… not sure he had real leadership capacity… not doing well in most aspects of his ministry.

I don't think I'd ever been hit as hard an emotional blow as this one… it just seemed to make no sense whatever, but for a few days I took it at face value. From my journal… *"so discouraged, hardest 24-48 hours of my life… feel like a totally broken person… cried more those next two days than all of maybe the last 10 years… in shower, @ leadership meeting, on phone, in bed, etc., etc. … feel like I weigh 400 lbs… all 4 corners of 1st floor of tall building crumbling."* I'm sure it was such an ego-shattering thing, and I took it so personally… felt I had been such a failure.

The local Committee asked Bob to come down… we met with him… then they told him I should stay… and Bob said ok. As the days went on, I began to realize a **hidden agenda**… (which he later admitted)… basically, that he differed with some of the decisions I had made, and so felt that I was not a team player. My journal… *"I feel very positive in my YL work recently… we* *are making great strides in a number of critical areas... but if I don't fit, or not wanted, or God has something else for us, I don't want to be in YL. It seems Bob has torn out a part of my heart for YL... feel I have many years of solid ministry ahead, Where?... where God wants me."*

Later on, Bob's hand-picked replacement told me, as did others... "you were doing exactly the right things for the Region."

* * * * * * * * * *

Days of Decision

I wasn't really sure what to do about my future, but prayed a good bit, talked with Patti, and then said to her **"We've got 10-20 good years left**, what do we want to do, that if we don't do it now, we'll miss out?" I could have stayed on in YL, but felt I didn't want to work with/under someone I had grown to not respect. (Many years later, Bob told a friend "I guess Bud is probably angry at me... and for good reason... "and I told him: **"I'm waiting for him to tell me that, but that's history, and I forgave him long ago."**)

So February 1st I resigned from YL... gave 6 months notice. I decided I wouldn't look for anything, nor listen to anyone, for 3 months... just pray and see what my heart says. During that time I said to Patti... **"you know, two-thirds of the world live and think differently from what we'll ever understand... let's get an education."** What I was basically thinking of was that perhaps we'd go to Central America for a year or two... work alongside the peons... see what we could learn, then return.

In returning from a year of teaching in Korea, Pete had come to Portland to live near us. I helped him get a job with World Concern, so he figured he'd reciprocate… help get **me** a job… and he told Art **Beals,** Executive Director of **World Concern**, that I was interested in something in the Third World. Art called, but I told him that I wasn't listening to anything until May 1ˢᵗ… so on May 1 he called, and asked if we'd come up to Seattle for an interview. There were a number of options he spoke of, but mainly **Bangladesh,** with the need for an Executive Director in a major agency there… and would we consider 4 years "**No.**" He persisted, but I kept saying no to the 4 years.

That summer of 1980 I was in Colorado for a month, finishing my graduate work, so was doing a lot of thinking, praying and writing re whatever was ahead. From my journal:

"In some ways I believe I could respond to the challenge of the Ex. Dir job —that I need a challenge virtually beyond me. But the biggest ? is what am I suited & gifted for — does that job fit me?… so now for me I face whether or not to stay in YL. I'm convinced I could make a good contribution, and have a whole new confidence that I could be extremely effective, but Bob tore out a big part of my heart for YL—it really has been hard at times to feel positive about the Mission. There was such a strong and almost violent expression on his part in asking for my termination, and obviously I still feel some of that, tho I know that God has graciously healed me of much of the personal hurt.

Now the ? is what about tomorrow? Where is my heart? I'm not totally sure, though I have felt that urge to do something overseas—specifically Third World. Somehow I want to make sure that this isn't merely a rational approach to a good-sounding idea—sounds really spiritual to want to identify w/ those with whom Christ would identify if he were here... but I really do want to do that which will be an expression of Jesus' life, and to have my own horizons stretched. I believe I would probably be stretched more by doing something different from YL—that for the next 10-20 years I can grow, & develop whole new parts of me.

But basically what I've been more aware of this week is that my own prayer life must increase tremendously—not spending enough time in S or prayer—so many things to hold before our Lord--that I don't come into God's presence often enough, don't pray enough for even the people I'm closest to — Patti & kids, etc. I simply need to be w/ God more, both in praise & intercession.

Yesterday we were in a study on sin and redemption, and last nite I was just meditating on it-- overwhelmed by God's grace in redemption—I am so unworthy, and so proud, and un-Christ-like, yet God has made me totally accepted by Him—hard to write how I felt—I just cried. Read a bit in the Psalms, then 1 Cor. 1—what a reminder, that my academic approach is absolute foolishness. It just seems so apparent that although there's no premium on ignorance, man's mind isn't what God uses nearly so much as his heart. Had a good time of prayer, especially felt good to pray for Bob, & really feel it. Wrote him today.

So the problem right now isn't the emotional part of leaving YL, but rather what specifically is God leading me to—feel both uncertainty and eagerness for whatever is ahead. Read Psalm 20, so good—"some trust in horses, but we trust in the name of the Lord our God." Lord, help me to have my trust in you for tomorrow--- not a job or organization... Oh God, teach me that Portland isn't my real home, that in your presence is where my security & home really is. Make me free enough to realize that all I have is not mine to 'own', but loaned as a gift from you, to be used for others. Now, how am I to live that out, both here &/or overseas. Make me free of 'things', that what I hold on to is you. Thank you, Lord, for your generosity—we have been so blessed. How can we take this & be your servants to/for those in such great need? God, lead us—we are yours.

Those 2 months in Colorado were most helpful, in being away from Portland while processing any decisions to be made. During that time I heard a song, **"Jesus Led Me All The Way"**, and wrote down the long list of how I felt God had led Patti and me:

> *We came on YL staff in '51, Philadelphia — <u>God was leading</u>*
> *Moved to Balto in '54 — <u>God was leading</u>*
> *Moved to D.C. in '58 — <u>God led us there</u>*
> *Sick in '60 — year off, to Palo Alto — <u>God was leading</u>, though seen in retrospect*
> *San Jose in '61 — <u>God led us there</u>*
> *To Detroit in '65?, but circumstances (H. S.) closed the door — <u>God led us step by step</u>*
> *To L.A. in '66 — <u>God led very specifically</u>*
> *To Chicago in '69 — <u>God was leading</u>*
> *To Portland in '78 — <u>God clearly led us again</u>*
> *… now in **1980 — God hasn't changed—He will lead!** O Lord, make me sensitive to your voice, for as a dumb sheep, I await your call, & want only to hear & respond to your voice. I am yours, in my weakness & strength. I trust you.*

During August, Bob Reeverts, head of YL's overseas ministries, asked me if we'd be interested in several overseas options… initially to provide some pastoring and training for **YL** staff in

South America—Peru in particular. I felt that could really fit into our interest in doing something internationally, and we pursued that—possibly go in September and October, by which time we'd know re Bangladesh. Lord, where?

* * * * * * * * * *

Around The World In 8 Days

In August Art Beals called and said "would you consider **3 years** (for Bangladesh), and could you **go to London for an interview in 3 weeks**?" I said yes to both, so Patti and I drove up to Seattle, where she would stay with my brother and his wife, while I would be gone to London for less than 48 hours.

I took my small briefcase... with just a book, change of shirt, socks and underwear... I'd be back the next day... and flew to **London**. Also being interviewed were two others... an Australian and an Englishman, for the position of Executive Director of **HEED Bangladesh** (**H**ealth, **E**ducation, **E**conomic **D**evelopment) a Christian Relief & Development consortium of 10 agencies, mostly European. The interview time was very thorough... 3 HEED Board men from 3 different continents... and later they said they were intrigued especially by the questions **I** had asked of them.

The next day, a couple of hours prior to my return flight, they said to me **"you're the one we want, but we don't want you to say 'yes' without seeing it... there's a plane leaving for Dacca in 2 hours ... can you go?"** So when Patti got a phone call in Seattle at **3 a.m.,** she knew it was me... I said I'd be home in 8 days.

The first leg was to Kuwait, on a 747… not very full, so I went upstairs… and the captain invited me into the cockpit, to see **Baghdad by night. W**hen I told him where I was headed he said: "you are going from one of the nicest places in the world to **the worst place in the world."** THANX! Then on to **Bombay,** for a hotel overnight. I knew I'd need a cotton shirt or two for the hot weather ahead, and they could have them made quickly, so this was my first time 'bargaining.' The price for 2 shirts?… "**115 rupees**", so I very astutely offered **100**. First mistake… I **should have said 40.** They knew they had me, and said "oh no, that's how much the material costs us." Oh well, I'm on **a huge learning curve**.

On to Calcutta the next day, and I was beginning to feel the discomfort of language limitations … incredibly crowded airports (no lines)… just getting to a hotel… heat… noise… being white… feeling so alone. Lying in bed that night in Calcutta I was apprehensive… what one feels on occasion when in a highly unusual situation… pinching one's self and saying **"what in the world am I doing here?"** Here I was, in **Calcutta … India…** how did I ever land there—3 days ago I was in Seattle, and now here???

I couldn't sleep… and having been told of foreigners being robbed in the middle of the night, even in a good hotel, I didn't take off my watch. So at 3 a.m. I decided to read… turned to resume my reading in Psalms, from The Living Bible… Chapter 67. Unbelievable!… "**send us around the world… for all mankind… throughout the earth… the nations**"… and more… "**Praise God, O world… all the peoples of the earth… peoples from remotest lands**"… !!! Only 7 verses in that short Psalm… and I immediately realized that this was **God…** taking me on a journey.

It was a short night, then on to Dacca… and getting off the plane I was hit by that oppressive **heat and humidity**. The current and interim Director, an Englishman (who had designed the arches in the Westminster Abbey), had numerous meetings for me, and I observed their laborious and excessive detail in all procedures… very British and proper… but **very little on the personal**. He was the 3rd Director in the 6 years of operation… with an expatriate staff of real professionals, from a dozen different countries, but with numerous areas of conflict along the way. Art had told me that HEED needed a '**healer and team-builder**', and I sensed why early on. I felt I had something to give, but was that for **me**? After 3 days there I headed home… 8 days around the world, with just my brief-case and $50, arrived home with **$40**… "don't leave home without it."

Now en route Tokyo/Seattle—feel a bit numb, but so anxious to see Patti—seems like a year. Last Mon. went to HEED office, then to see projects. Dacca camps unbelievable—20,000 in 12-13 acre plot, all under tin roofs—open sewage, recent floods had everything under 2 feet of water.

During the 3 days, and now, such feelings, zenith to nadir, from 'no way' to 'I could really bring something to them.' Having left I just begin to be aware of how little I really understand where to start—feel helpless and rather inadequate, especially re the cultural thing. Could contribute mainly to staff in personal and pastoral ways, and also in some admin ways—the staff hadn't done their homework on much of the stuff—also, they need to be together more for spiritual and ministry R&D –the 2 days are exclusively business except for a 20 minute devotional.

Well God, what are you saying? A part of me is saying how great it would be if Art in Seattle said "no way." Can I really take Patti there? —my stomach sinks when I think of it from the factor of living conditions. The job is complicated and varied—at the same time, much of what the Board wants is up-front stuff—p r, caring, churches, funding, etc. Feelings go to extremes—even re the overall ministry. Seems hopeless and futile in so many ways—only a drop in the ocean, and seems no end in sight—prognosis not encouraging. At the same time, perhaps only through <u>many</u> years of ministering to human needs in Jesus' name will the Gospel take form—also, Jesus says to do it any way—Matt. 25. Right now my heart just swells inside me—I want to cry—is it for those people? Or that I/we may end up going? Don't know, but I do know I've seen the tip of the iceberg in terms of human need. Now Lord, what am I to do?

I arrived back in Seattle mid-Sept., and asked Art when he needed an answer... "by noon October 1" he said, and I told him I'd let him know the morning of Oct. 1. **Patti** was sure it would not be the easiest place for a woman, and had some real reservations... "**Bangladesh???**" As we prayed during those next couple of weeks, neither of us felt any clear direction, and Patti still had real qualms... I told her that if she didn't want to go, we wouldn't go... so we sat down and listed pros and cons:

Pro	Con
Learn from Third World culture	*Time gone – 3 yrs? our kids*
Minister to needs of the poor	*Coping/change... vocation, geo., climate, age*
Job description fits	*No strong affirmation from friends*

Misc. circumstances	Handle language???
Compatibility w/ WC vision	Patti/family communication
Prepare for future	Travel costly

We were asking ourselves questions, such as the best use of our gifts/experience… how best to develop spiritual formation… wanting that in which we could both be involved… could we really make a difference in such a totally different environment, etc.

The morning of October 1 came, and I didn't have the slightest idea of what I would say to Art. Then 2 totally different but equally amazing things happened. First, as I was praying, asking the Lord for clarity**… yes or no?**… it was almost like a voice, God saying "**it doesn't really make any difference, Bud… you can say 'yes' or 'no', and either one will be ok… so long as my honor is your commitment, I will bless you.**"

What an incredible release and freedom came over me. Instead of a lot of navel-gazing as to God's will, it was so clear that what He was saying was '**you're a big boy, Bud… what does your *heart* want to do?… and if that honors me, I will bless you.**' So at that point I didn't know whether it would be a yes or no, but there was a real freedom of spirit.

Then the **second** amazing thing occurred, but first… … back in **April**, we had a special speaker at our church, one of maybe two top leaders in the American Church on Islamic culture. At the end of his talk, our pastor had us stand and sing… "**Freely, freely, you have received, freely, freely, give**… " As we were singing, my insides felt as if I was **literally** on fire… never felt anything like that, ever… felt so weird… what was that all about? But I never thought about it again.

Then, six months later, on the morning of **October 1**, Patti woke up **singing**… **"Freely, freely, you have received, freely, freely, give"**… and she then turned to have her devotions, picking up on where she had left off the day before, in Matthew 10. The first words she read were **"Freely you have received, freely give…** "She called over to me and said, "**honey, I think we should go.**"

Later on, after I had said yes… they sent me the application for the position… one of the questions being "What is your experience in development?" Of course I had had a good bit of experience in this, having been responsible in YL for major **fund development**. I didn't realize until much later that in the Third World **'development'** has little to do with money… it has to do with elevating the level of the **'have-nots.'** I'm sure there were questions raised in some minds… do we have the right guy?

During that Fall of 1980, while we were awaiting all the details of a 'foreign investment,' I went to Pasadena for 2 weeks to take the last course in my graduate work. I decided to not go for the M.Div., as in going to a Muslim country, I didn't want a 'religious' degree… also felt the same in an increasingly secular society. So my M.A. from Fuller Seminary is in Theology and Counseling.

Foreign
Investments

CHAPTER 10

GETTING THERE/ENTRY

After such a clear sense of God's leading, the next 7 months were most uncomfortable. HEED had said that our visas would probably come by December, which gave us ample time for preparation and the move, but along the way came numerous government delays, and by January it was getting a bit frustrating. I had continued my work in YL, but for Patti the days just grinded on... February... March... so we decided we would put out the **'fleece'. O**n April 1 we decided that if the visas didn't come by **April 16**, my birthday, it was a sign that we weren't supposed to go. **On April 15 the visas came**... we sold our home the next week, and left Portland a few days later. We asked for prayer that **all** of our luggage would go through... apparently not uncommon upon arrival for them to go through **everything**... sometimes help themselves... but they **only opened one**... most unusual.

Prior to leaving the States I wrote a letter to our 4 children... telling them of our love for them, and some general considerations in case something happened to us. **Cherie was in Tucson** with her 2 girls... **Pete** was in **Malaysia,** working with Vietnamese 'boat people'... **Phil** was just finishing at **Florida Institute of**

Technology… and **Steve** was at the **U. of Oregon**. Pete wrote in a letter that he and **Linda Evans** wanted to get engaged… so could we come through Kuala Lumpur on our way… which we did. And what fun that was… to host an engagement dinner. But it was also bittersweet, as we had hoped to have some extended time with them… but we could only have 2 days, as we had to get to Dacca quickly for the start of the new language class.

Sat. nite hard, we both cried a good bit—feeling cheated in only 2 days w/ P&L—that all Patti's life she was looking forward to a daughter-in-law, & now w/ such a special one as Linda, it was as though we were given a priceless gift, only to have it taken away. Is God really good? & fair? We know He is, but right now it hurts. Left Sun. a.m. amid great tears… a long lonely flight to Bangkok.

The first night in Dacca was one of those memorable ones… sleeping for the first time under a **mosquito net**… one of the worst nights of our lives. We didn't know that we were supposed to tuck the net **under** the mattress, and **100 mosquitos** sent their friends the message… "**fresh meat**." Ugh! We never again slept under a net… used a **spray** in the room… used **smoke coils** that gave a repellent odor… and especially when up country would rub on **Muskol**, a very effective repellent.

The well-known author and speaker, **Tom Sine**, tells the story about mosquito nets in one of his books. Our first year there he stayed with us in Dacca for an overnight… and upon retiring, he asked about "**no mosquito net**" in his room. I assured him that all was ok… that we had sprayed, and then gave him the bottle of Muskol. The next morning he said it was an absolutely **horrible** night… he had applied the Muskol to his arms, turned off the light, and heard bzzz... **swat**... bzzz... **swat**... bzzz ... turned on the light, swatted mosquitos, then light off, and bzzz... **all night.** I said "that can't be... let me see the bottle." Sure enough, it was the **Muskol** bottle... but then I said "**oh no**... that bottle was **empty,** and I had put **shampoo** in it for when I went up country." He said he had wondered why it seemed to lather up when he applied it.

* * * * * * * * * *

Learning Bangladesh

We started language school... 4 hours each morning, then practicing it outside with whomever... and, combined with moving into our own flat, life felt thrown at us. We had a Bengali cook, who spoke a little bit of English, and our Bihari cleaning lady (**aya),** who knew none (the Bihari's are **Pakistani refugees**, living in a **refugee camp** (see book cover photo)... not allowed to return to Pakistan after the 1971 war of independence from W. Pakistan... no one lower in Bangladesh). The flat was not clean... no lights in 2 of the 3 rooms, so we ate by candle light.

Friday we had a Bengali lunch at school, sitting on the floor, & eating w/ our hands—not easy, and hot food. First wash hands w/ water poured over a bucket, & end same. I had terrible back pains and had to go home to bed... ... by Sunday I couldn't even stand up, and in bed couldn't even turn over... ... Wed. the 20ᵗʰ went to hospital to be fitted for a brace, ready Fri. Amid all this the Lord gave me Psalm 94:19... but feel overwhelmed, as tho I'm going down for the 3ʳᵈ time ... the heat, no lites or electricity Sun. afternoon & nite, and no water since. Having to learn what it means to cope, & get along w/ bare essentials. But, it feels right to be here, & we are aware of God's love & presence. And we have each other... ... Oh Lord, make my heart like yours, to see people as you see them, & not concerned about my comforts or circumstances.

It has been 3 weeks since we left, and already there are so many things that, although tedious or uncomfortable, are a part of everyday living...
- *feeling sticky an hour after a shower*
- *lizards on the walls (they're good—eat the bugs)*
- *2"cockroaches everywhere (they're bad—eat everything)*
- *the traffic, cars 1 or 2 abreast coming right at us, on our side*
- *95 degrees days, 80 at nite*
- *a week of no hot water*
- *mosque <u>loud</u>speaker call to prayer 5x day, starts at 4:30 am*
- *rickshawing amid the wild traffic*
- *ceiling fans going constantly, especially while asleep*

Some Bengali facts & customs...
- *only 18% literate—no more than sign name*
- *no touching in public (ok w/ same sex)*
- *stare — England, 1 sec. —America, 5 sec. —here, 1hour*
- *burp is good, "ate up to his neck"*
- *not point or touch w/ left hand, unclean*
- *mind & heart, same place*
- *don't usually say "no" or "I don't know"... save face, so "I'll try", or "I can't say*
- *not say "thank you", "excuse me"*
- *75% of children malnourished*
- *15% death rate by age 1, 25% by age 5*
- *80% cannot read or write their name*

I still lie here with a bad back… really discouraged, but can get caught up on reading & meditation. Reading Utmost for His Highest each a.m… so good and apropos this a.m… mainly feel badly for Patti, as she feels the load of all—cook & aya, no water for 5 days, no transport, etc. And the heat can be so enervating, she's not sleeping well, and the 4:30 a.m. loudspeaker call to prayer every morning is an automatic alarm clock… noises never cease. Patti was told that the water on occasion runs between 2-5 a.m., so she took a 2 a.m. shower.

There were about 20,000 Biharis living in a 12-13 acre plot, all on one level… no sanitation, cardboard for walls, sewage running freely… and that is where our aya lived. She invited Patti and me to her 'home', a 10x10 confine, in which she, her disabled husband, and 4 children lived.

6/20 We were overwhelmed that she would invite us… our car was mobbed by children… they had rented or borrowed a table & 3 chairs… their boys had shirts on, the only boys w/ shirts of the scores we saw there… & they served us pineapple, bananas, & a snack food. We took some of that, but didn't drink any of the water poured into the 3 glasses. What a great time it was! The temperature <u>outside</u> was 100, and as soon as we entered they began to fan us— as they said in very broken English "aiyer cawndeeeshun". None can speak any English, & of course our Bangla is very limited—but we really communicated. When we left we could hardly get through the crowds of kids—they literally surrounded us—some had never seen a white person. It was a great motivator to learn the language, and a great time.

6/28 Patti was quite sick for 4 days—fever, vomiting, diarrhea, etc… ok now… life seems so laborious in just routine things—some humorous. Our phone hasn't been working for 2-3 weeks—the guy came today, & apparently when the front doorbell was repaired the men wired the phone wires to the doorbell. On occasion we have our moments of sadness, & of missing our friends & children. I realize how much I feel Patti's being ill—everything becomes discolored.

7/4 After an 11 hour train ride from Dacca, we arrived at Kamalganj yesterday… only 8 miles from India… then a "4ᵗʰ" picnic for all bideshis (foreigners) *down at the 'lake'—made by HEED 2 years ago. Went swimming—warm, dirty, nice… returned to shower, and later when I saw blood all over the floor, noticed bleeding… from a leech on the bottom of my foot… removed by our Finnish Dr.*

* * * * * * * * * *

New On the Job

8/23 My first 3 weeks on the job, at the office—Executive Director, HEED B'desh—really felt comfortable, which I guess surprised me. And I sensed a good response from the 'nationals.' But I have so much to learn about the org., about the culture, etc. Pete & Linda came a week ago—what a joy—we spent a day of getting caught up. Friday Patti went w/ them to **Calcutta***, to see* **Mother Theresa's** *work—Patti came back with* **"Calcutta, what a breath of fresh air!"** (Compared to the Muslim culture in Bangladesh, how true that was, we both learned.)

9/5 Friday nite took train to Kamalganj—arrived about 6:30 a.m., to be greeted by about 20 HEED staff. Sat. afternoon they had a huge reception/party for us—150-200 staff, from miles around— speeches, plaques, entertainment, etc.--& I spoke, via an interpreter.

Monday with Dr. Steve Brown & some of his health staff… they train gov't health workers… hope to increase their weekly work hours from 10% to 30%… hope to have enough success so that the govt. program will be seen for what it is… gov't talks big, good reports, but 0 happening. Then went to see a tube well, through the mud, & ended up barefoot, with mud over ankles, pants rolled to knees. Most of their drinking water is from stagnant ponds—15% die by age 1, 25% by age 5… mainly from lack of clean water or clean health facilities, which results in scabies, TB, worms, anemia, malnutrition, diarrhea, hepatitis, etc.

Just a few hours at our HEED Leprosy Hospital gave me a month full of things to thank God for; I watched our beautiful Dr. Cochrane, Director of the hospital, performing a tendon transplant on a fifteen-year-old boy, and without which the young lad would have had a lifetime of increasing uselessness of his hands. Observed the toeless man who, after an operation, can now walk for the first time in years. Saw the fingerless leper teaching others to knit; many whose fingers were half gone, but who now had something to do with what they had left. Watched as an old man was being bandaged daily by one of the world's numberless Mother Theresas.

After an entire week of visiting most all of HEED's Kamalganj projects — *What about all this-----?*

My wildest imagination would never have thought 18 mo. ago that one day I/we would actually be doing what we have seen in occasional missionary pictures—sitting in mud huts w/ thatched roof, eating their food, walking barefoot through ankle-deep mud (where the animals add to the flavor), crossing streams on 3" bamboo "bridges" & also wading thru them, drinking warm milk from the cow in the next room & tea made from pond water where the animals drink & bathe, touching leper patients, etc. etc. But how similar this seems to the culture of Jesus' day, and it has made the Scriptures so much more alive & real. We see how narrow has been our scope of what's going on in the world—obviously my tendency has been to want more creature comforts and to be concerned re security, etc. Here, it's day-to-day existence, with virtually no creature comforts. Yet the people do not complain & they seem basically happy.

I don't know how this could relate to life back in the States, the status search there, the need for comfort, always wanting more of everything... ... does the introduction of our technology & methods inevitably lead to change of their culture? Our tendency is to send & provide extensive funds for building churches or other institutions & programs, & thus the people will need to have our continued $ & other support in order to maintain what we have introduced. How can we assist them without the inflow of substantial sums of $, which keeps them on 'welfare.' The Bangladesh Church must come to the place where it ministers to the needs of the poor, even out of its' own poverty.

9/18 Told Patti this a.m. that I felt as though I had re-entered the rat race. It doesn't feel good, & I'm exhausted—maybe just the pressure of having to get all the Board stuff in the mail by today. Right now I'm on the "Rocket", a 24 hr old-boat river ride to Dacope, after ½ hour plane to Jessore, then 2 hour bumpy bus to Khulna... but I have not felt good physically at times, blood count is 34, & Dr. not sure what the problem is... anemia?... lost 25 lbs, really feel sluggish & lethargic at times. My times w/ the Lord have been less regular... this & my tiredness may be factors in my feeling the futility of being here—am a bit discouraged & discombobulated. I need more focus—at times wish we weren't here—miss the kids and friends back home. Hate to return home in Nov. for Pete & Linda wedding, for as Patti says, probably won't want to come back here. Need strong input from our Lord — feel dry.

10/25 Wow! More than a month, & soooo much has happened. Just read the above, & one good thing is that I have had some great times in Scripture this last month. Just tonite read in Luke 11 re "you love the front seats of the synagogue"—here the most important man sits in the front row. Had a good week in Dacope—hot! Travel is by water, so each day on the 'tug' to a different village. Tues. we walked about 5 miles in 110 degree weather—on one occasion thru mud literally above our ankles, & at one point I stepped into a pile of manure & lost my sandal a foot deep into it—had to fish for it & then wash it off in the river.

Well----the whole matter of bribery, corruption, dishonesty, etc. is so widespread here that it almost makes us want to vomit, or go home, or something. We have had 2 'Christian' accountants fired earlier this year. I asked Jim Mckinley, 23 yrs here, if this is unusual, & he said "no", that every org. has the same… every person is on the take. What an education! Oh yes, an interesting comment from our bldg supt.—"shouldn't you pay more for honesty?" On the matter of bribery, after about 6 months in B'desh, Patti told me that she thought our cook, a 'Christian', was taking money… we had to give him $ almost every day to buy food… so I asked Jim Mckinley about that, and he said "of course… if you're getting away with less than 10% you're better off than most of us."

12/25 So much water under the bridge since I last wrote here—last Friday we had our Dacca staff party, & all said it was the best ever—about 125-150 for a program & dinner. Good! Then last nite, Christmas eve, we had 20+ adults & 10 children here for dinner… they loved it. What do we do to make our 1ˢᵗ Christmas away from home enjoyable??—invite Bengalis. So we arranged to have them for today, and then open house for all HEED staff— many seemed eager.

So after a good Christmas eve with expats, today was all Bengalis — breakfast with Shakeel & Ramdash & then to Immanuel church with them & Hasheem & Jogodisch & Mele. That's 2 converted Muslims,1 Hindu, & a tribal girl… all 5 of whom spent the day with us. After playing truth/consequences and other games, we sang some carols, then prayed & talked, & then had evening meal & dessert… they were with us all day, 9-9 or 10, & really felt it was special—their first Christmas as Christians.

12/29 Yesterday Sylvester and a friend came by… helpful chat to see things from their perspective. The new generation of Christians only go thru the 10ᵗʰ grade & then get jobs in Christian organizations to support their family. We need to establish a scholarship fund to assist bright & committed kids to go thru HSC, B.A, & M.A.

1/1/82 What a year 1981 was. Now this past week has been a roller coaster inside, as there are times when I feel that we absolutely can't make a difference here—the system is so corrupt, & it seems hopeless… all predictions for the future are pessimistic. The one thing we hang on to is that we are here by God's appt., and that He wants an expression of Himself in every culture, regardless of the response… what an opportunity to see if God can make something of this virtual nothing. We see the difference in some of these young people… they feel they're being treated as persons rather than as 'lessers'. Yesterday one of the staff wives told Patti that the staff at the Dacca Camps are so happy about an E.D. who shows interest in them… that it is so different now from before.

The struggle I guess is that it just seems to take so much more effort to be loving & caring, amid so many adverse & negative circumstances & situations. The whole atmosphere of poverty, filth, beggars, corruption, robbers (2 out of 3 nites this week we had them in & thru our property)… it makes life seem such a struggle & so enervating.

This morning I took 3 Bangladeshis to Immanuel church, and at the end of the service Simon Sharkar asked all to stand who wanted to commit themselves to God's service for '82. Shakeel told me what he was saying, & asked if I wanted to stand… it was obvious that he wanted to stand, & wanted to do that with me, so I stood… & he stood. As I was standing during prayer I was looking down at our hands, resting on the chairs in front of us—my light skin next to his dark brown skin, and a million thoughts raced through my mind…

- *what a rich gift God has given me to experience in advance a small bit of corporate praise around His throne from "every tribe & nation"*
- *just the amazement of being here ½ way around the world — still seems unreal at times*
- *one in Christ w/ all people*
- *Shakeel's love for me, & servant spirit, and his leadership potential*
- *to give myself to Christ for '82 with a Bangladeshi.*

Later on I wrote… *Having helped Shakeel get a new job at Shetuli, I then took him to get some shoes, as he would need those working at our HEED shop in the 5-star Sonargaon Hotel… he has never worn a pair in his life. We went to several stores, didn't have his size, & then found one. He tried them on, looked down at them on his feet, thought they looked preposterous, kicked them off & said he didn't like or need them. The changes required of these people are too much sometimes.*

On occasion I feel such a heaviness of heart — what have we done to westernize people. Every Bengali Christian leader w/ whom I have spoken has talked about how much all the $ has hurt them— made them dependent, greedy, corrupt, etc. How much of the great outpouring of funds comes as a result of the need for a relief agency to have marketable data—that which can be used to raise more $ & which makes them look so good in the eyes of many back home. What should we do in HEED that will not perpetuate dependency – only God can give us the insights we need.

* * * * * * * * * *

One of my early mistakes as Executive Director was with Lou, who had been the acting director... that he should keep the good car, and I would take the lesser... wanting to show a **servant spirit.** But I didn't realize how confusing this was to staff... who really is E.D.? So after a month we switched, but I had to figure out how to really show servanthood in a culture where everything is top down. So I suggested to Patti what we would do... we'd start by inviting our headquarters staff to our home for lunch ... and **we would serve them...** first have the management group. But then the second week I deliberately went down the ladder... to the bottom, and had the **peons...** that was their job title... the ones who cleaned the toilets, etc. And **Patti and I served them** lunch in our home. They just couldn't believe it, and over time many said they had never been treated like this in their lives.

Interestingly… on the above occasion with the peons… and at other times with others… when they left, there were **footprints on the toilet seat**. Their normal latrine would be a hole in the ground… or, as even on the trains, a hole in the floor… so what else does one do with what they've never seen.

CHAPTER 11

WHY ARE WE HERE?

Sat. Jan. 23 Time is flying, & have been extremely busy this month... set up a 2-day meeting with all our expats to discuss our future in HEED — response has been amazing... "Who cares what HEED looks like in 3 years?" Etc. It will not be an easy thing to get them to think in terms of anything other than doing their own thing. So much of what I hear & see leaves me so uncertain as to what can really be effective here in development work — i.e., how to not help the rich get richer but to help the really poor... so much benefit to those in power, including the Church.

In the 2 days with the expat staff I had asked a number of questions re our future... and didn't find them really helpful in looking at the long-term effects of our presence in the country. Even though we had some world experts in their respective fields... health... agriculture... education... engineering — good Christians, but most did not understand a **Kingdom agenda.** They were there with good hearts, and wanted to give service to the poor... true altruism, but rather narrow vision.

I decided that I needed to meet with a group of **national** leaders... Bengali Christians who could help give me a perspective from the local point of view… and how **they** saw HEED. I met with 7 or 8 of them together for a morning… a doctor, a professor at Dacca U., the national head of YMCA, et al. I asked some of the same questions I had asked the expats… one of which was "If HEED had to leave in 6 months, what would we do differently?" The answer came back quickly and pointedly… *"**Good! Why do you want to wait 6 months!** And take all your missionaries with you. It may mean we'd have to go back to driving rickshaws, but at least it may show the Christian for what he should be."* Another said: *"we are seen by the dominant culture as **little Europeans,** as **2nd & 3rd class citizens.**"* Ouch!!! And they were dead serious… I obviously had a lot to learn. But in my not being a 'missionary', they felt free to speak more candidly… said they appreciated my openness to them.

Through the next year or so I asked many persons, at all levels… church, business, government … Minister of Education, Minister of Health, etc… "**Where is the hope in Bangladesh?**" Much to my surprise… 100% said "**there is none.**" Now what do I do with that?… and had to wrestle within myself as to why we were there… HEED, the largest development agency in the country, with **70 expert expats** (& **200 Muslims** on staff)… can we make a difference? I concluded that the Christian nationals had a love/hate relationship with missionaries… most grateful for what they brought… but also were usually made to feel 'lesser', and dependent on outsiders.

Over a period of time, I realized that our task was not to somehow 'salvage' Bangladesh… and that ministering in/to the Muslim world was a most formidable task… but that God desires His person and love to be expressed to every person in the world… that we were there as a living witness to His grace, and we could leave any response to that up to Him. We would simply be **salt and light,** in one of the darkest corners of the world. I could relax. (How does one relax in Bangladesh?)

* * * * * * * * * *

Highs and Lows

Feb 10 The last few days have been some of the heaviest emotionally that I've had—not sure I understand all that's going on inside, but I even got sick—fever, chills, etc., & had felt so tense & tight physically & emotionally... ... In the process of all this I was discovering at least 2 things — 1) I think I've just discovered I'm the Ex. Dir... have not been seeing HEED from a top down perspective, & just relating mechanically to issues as they arose... and thinking 'what would Lou do?' Since I know so little about HEED, development, culture, etc., I've not felt I could be assertive, & in fact was probably being intimidated by Lou... a couple of days of considerable depression—about as much as maybe I've ever had... but 2) I think I've finally "lit" —I'm really here, & I see now that the task has not been clear in my mind... still getting acclimated, & settling in to being in Asia, doing administration, not management. So today I'm taking a day off here at the SB guest house—I need this so much.

*A very busy 2 weeks, & this week at the Dacca Convention. Last nite Jim McKinley spoke... "**AS** the Father has sent me—so send I you" **AS** – the way of suffering, loneliness, rejection, etc. Said he wasn't interested in going on a tour to see Israel —"don't you want to walk where Jesus walked?"... "No, I want to walk where he is walking... exotic tours go to Israel, but not to B'desh, or Haiti, or... "an act of the will, to give up what is mine by birth & by* *right... what went through the mind of God the Son when He deliberated on leaving heaven — "Out of the Ivory Palaces, Into a World of Woe."*

Mar 14 An absolutely exhausting & taxing 2+ weeks, especially with the evaluators here... they have examined us from A to Z, and the result is some pretty devastating stuff. They asked me "how well do you feel you have taken the reins?" & I said very poorly, that I have been extremely frustrated both in terms of the nature of HEED & in relationship to Lou. These 2 weeks have put me on the biggest roller coaster I've ever been on — extreme lows & a few real highs. Never in my life have I felt so inadequate—not knowing dev. work, or HEED, & seeing what HEED really needs is a whole restructuring of the org., needs a management systems analyst. And that obviously isn't me.

In the process I've acknowledged to God my helplessness in all this, & that if any good was going to come about it would be due to His grace & generosity, not my ability. The amazing thing has been that I began to come up with some of the things that are probably exactly the kinds of approaches we need, mainly in the area of organizational re-structuring & admin. procedures... and developed a format & plan for a long-range planning procedure for defining goals & objectives

That provided me with a real feeling of accomplishment, but at the same time the total awareness that it was God doing this thru me, that it wasn't the usual me. But it felt good, & I was fully aware that it was God — & He was carrying me <u>day by day</u>. I readily acknowledged <u>each day</u> my inadequacy, that for that day He'd meet me. What a tremendous mixed emotion—that God really was carrying me, I was <u>feeling</u> the strength—but also the *feeling that tomorrow wasn't assured—only today. That meant I couldn't go into tomorrow with assurance… self-assurance, that is. So humbling! For years I've expressed to my staff that "God never gives us that which we're capable of doing— He gives us that which is beyond us, & then gives us Himself to accomplish it." Although I've experienced this in rather small ways in the past, never even close to what this has been. He has given me what I am absolutely incapable of handling, & the only way it's going to get done is by His grace & strength as I readily acknowledge day by day my own inadequacy. It's been amazing to see those days & times when I've felt absolutely challenged & exhilarated by the awareness of feeling directed specifically. For the first time I've felt comfortable as the E.D. Thank you, Lord, for your generosity to me these past days.*

CHAPTER 12

BACKGROUND, CHALLENGE AND CHANGE

India was under British rule, but under great pressure from the Muslim sector, in 1947 they divided the country... arbitrarily drew vertical lines in both the east and west, some right through the middle of towns... creating a **new country**, consisting almost exclusively of **Muslims**... and **East** & **West Pakistan** was formed ... **one country, 1000 miles apart.** Riots occurred all over India between Muslims & Hindus, with up to half a million killed, and **24 million refugees**. One person had said "if you do this, within 10 years **East Pakistan** will become the **cesspool of the world.**" (It's an area 2/3 the size of Oregon, with 150 million population today, with almost no natural resources.) Then in 1971 East Pakistan declared a war of independence... and **Bangladesh** came into existence.

As we have all learned since, Bangladesh is a tragedy waiting to happen... tornadoes, floods, tidal waves, etc... they happen every year, and some will remember the tidal wave of 1974, in which half a million Bengalis were drowned in one tidal wave, and a U.S. rock group sponsored "**Bangladesh,**" which raised millions for relief. It was then that a number of Christian agencies got together, and agreed that instead of all of them going individually to help, they would take on the form of the United Mission to Nepal, where all mission agencies work together under one umbrella. So **HEED Bangladesh** was formed… 10-12 Christian agencies, mostly European (2 U.S., World Concern & MAP). Many of these agencies had operations in other parts of the world, so development experts came from probably 15 countries… doctors, nurses, agronomists, engineers, administrators, etc.

The challenge, of course, became that of having such a disparate group of people working together. HEED grew quickly, and with major projects in several different parts of the country, the task was to develop an infrastructure that would have all these people on the same page. Within 4 years they had 2 different Executive Directors, and then an interim one, and then looking for… whomever. I saw early on why one of the things mentioned to me in the interview was the need for a 'healer.'

I think that our years in YL were of great help, with a major focus on **relationships**… and especially the nationals received us so well. We saw that so many expats have their primary focus on their task, not on people… and we've learned and experienced since, what many expats have said… that it's often easier to relate to the nationals than to many from different mission agencies. So for me the initial challenge was to **learn the culture** and **learn development** … but here I was, a novice on both, among a group of experts. "Lord… HELP!"

I began to read up on the area of development, and was determined to discover how HEED could become a major force

for change in assisting the have-nots… was primarily taken with **Ghandi's** approach, in which he states 3 main steps:
- uplift of spirit
- preservation of the culture
- provide for one's own needs

Dec. 12 Last week a group from Sweden was here to see what was happening in the country re development… met w/ the directors of misc. agencies… I spent 2 hours w/ them. This evening at a reception for them, the head guy came up to me & said that the group unanimously had voted that mine was their best session in their 2 weeks, & they want me to come to Sweden for a week-10 days to lecture on dev… they want good input to the Swedish Gov't, Parliament, Church, etc. What a stitch!! I had to literally bite my tongue to keep from laughing. Who knows less about dev. than I? I guess from what one of them told Patti it was the attitude of not having all the answers, & getting to the heart of defining what ?s needed to be asked that impressed them.

I think that what happened… most of the agencies showed them what they were <u>doing</u>… I told them what I was <u>learning.</u> I asked them to put into writing their goals & expectations of such a visit… sounded so very official… but no way am I going to go, only to embarrass me and them both, since they already have heard everything I know.

But I was learning enough to realize that we really should pursue **nationalization of HEED**… that **nationals** needed to own and run it… not foreigners. So at the Board meeting that Spring I asked if I could present a plan for the Fall meeting that would lead toward that, and they approved. The next 6 months was one of the most challenging of my 4 years there…

first, how to convince the nationals that they **could** do it... and succeed. And then to show them **how** they could do it. But their mentality was '**white** is right... we're too **corrupt**... we're not capable... won't get funding', etc.

So I began by inviting 7 or 8 of the national Christian leaders for a day of discussion. We went to a Chinese restaurant for lunch, and one said: "you go ahead and order, Mr. Bylsma", and I told them "no, you order for yourselves." "No, you order for all of us", and I responded as before. Then **Dr. Chowdhury**, superintendent of the big hospital in Chittagong, took the menu, and ordered for everyone... **now I knew who their real leader was.**

Basically, I laid out a plan in which the next year the HEED Board would consist of at least **60%** nationals... I wanted them to have majority input right from the get-go... the next year **80%,** and the following year **100%.** I suggested that they would have to focus on 3 primary areas... the **spiritual**, in **development,** and in **management**... that if we failed in any one of those, it wouldn't work. So I set up a plan for having a number of key staff to get studies in these areas... (we had about 25 staff who already had a M.A. degree)... to India, England, Australia, Philippines, etc... didn't want any to go to the U.S., as those who do so often never return. The nationals were feeling so strongly affirmed, in our wanting them to take leadership... and later on I would suggest to Terril Eikenberry, who become my successor, that he needed to be the last expat as Executive Director.

That Fall the Board unanimously approved our proposal... and it was **a new future for HEED**... but for me some new challenges in walking through many complicated areas. Would it work?... almost every agency said it wouldn't... said: **"you're crazy."**

* * * * * * * * * *

"They Shall Walk (or ride) **and not Faint"**

In a place like Bangladesh, just to maintain an ordinary day's effort... at work or home... one faces so many potential pitfalls, obstacles, struggles. The weather, corruption at all levels, the inept systems, and so much more... makes it so easy to often be off balance... and my having had **malaria twice** and **dysentery** many times didn't help. So many things seem to operate against normal living as we would know it in the States... plus the tremendous cultural differences, not only ours from that of the nationals, but even the differences within the expat community.

* * * * * * * * * *

May 5 Postponed my trip to Kamalganj due to malaria, and then infected toes... also had a terrible ear infection, first left then right... 10 days of antibiotics, finally relief but still muffled hearing. Feels like the "dark night of the soul" these last months — not close to the Lord, detached, not much praying, alone or w/ Patti, not motivated, most thoughts on returning to the States — and it's a _long_ way away yet. Patti discouraged somewhat, maybe because I'm down.

The feelings of helplessness, frustration, inadequacy—at times close to despair—all these and more are not uncommon but apparently consistent with the experience of most others who come here. There seems to be an insidious subtlety of hopelessness that is so pervasive, and rarely do we hear much expression of hope or optimism. "Hope deferred makes the heart sick"—but what of little or no hope at all???

* * * * * * * * * *

We went to Mr. Kahn's dinner party—I forgot my camera, so drove home to get it. On the way I felt deep, sharp twinges in my heart area, different from what I've ever felt before, and it felt as though it would go at any moment... also a funny physical feeling which I can't explain. But thoughts of my father and brother Perk, who both died instantly of a heart attack, raced through my mind. I really thought this might be the end for me.

As I was driving I thought how terribly inconvenient it would be for Patti—no ID, it could be hours or longer to find me, plus the horrible problem of winding up affairs here... all alone. So I told the Lord that I was certainly ready to go, but that for Patti's sake to 1) let me get to the house at least, 2) if it pleased Him to wait until we were together, & 3) wait till we were back in the States. "Lord, please, for Patti's sake, wait until a more favorable time — remember her, your daughter." I was trying to think of where there was a Dr., to whose house I could drive, but kept heading back to the house. Got here ok, walked slowly inside, and gradually felt no more chest pain, nor the other ominous feeling. Felt good, and drove back to the party... ... Once again, life seems so <u>temporary</u>, and so it must not be grasped at but enjoyed. Oh God, give me the capacity to love you, embrace you, embrace life, w/ abandon, w/ zest. And thank you for a wife who loves me as I am.

It was rather amazing to experience such extreme highs and lows during our years there. But there were enough times of experiencing God's intervention and strength… we could "walk & not faint."

* * * * * * * * * *

Bangladesh Potpourri

I had to make an occasional trip to Europe, to maintain touch with our agencies and funding sources. One trip in particular was intriguing. I had been to England, then Holland, and on to **Germany…** a 2 ½ hour drive at 100+ mph on the autobahn, where I was with Bread for the World for a couple of days. The director, Jorg Isert, was taking me to the Stuttgart airport, and I told him how good it was to be back in Germany again… "everything is so beautiful… so efficient, and we Americans tend to forget how much we learned from Germany… **and can still learn**." He asked me: "do you really believe that?" and I said: "yes, I do." To which he replied: "**So does every German!**"

* * * * * * * * * *

On one of our trips up to Kamalganj, when we arrived they told us of Elgin Saha having been bitten on the foot the night before by a **cobra… usually deadly**. His wife quickly told one of the Bengali health workers… a former Hindu but now a Christian… to get the doctor… quickly. HEED had several doctors there, including Ian Cochrane at the leprosy hospital. So the health worker ran down the hill… and notified the **witch doctor**… who came up with a large number of his cohorts… all crowding and chanting in this small room. The witch doctor put 2 or 3 tourniquets around his leg, and then made a cut into his foot, with very dark blood coming out. He said "**see, those are the evil spirits coming out.**"

When we heard of this, we went quickly to see Elgin, and felt that perhaps we should exorcise any evil spirits who might have lingered there. Elgin told us that while the witch doctor and his friends were in the room, that Dr. Cochrane poked his head inside the room... **but did nothing.** When I talked with him the next day, he told me that after a witch doctor has done his thing on someone, he would **never** do anything following that... that if the person were to die, the village would blame him.

That evening Patti and I went to Elgin's home to pray... laid our hands on his very swollen and purple foot ... praying that any lingering evil spirits would depart. Afterward, Elgin's wife, Theresa, said "did you see that brilliant **shaft of light coming through the ceiling**... right onto Elgin's foot?"

* * * * * * * * * *

Charlton Heston was in town to do a documentary for a mission agency, and the media arranged for a speech at the 5-star Sonargaon Hotel. The agency director asked Patti and me to join him, his wife, and Heston and his wife and daughter, for dinner afterward... basically he wanted to have an American to help with the conversation. It wasn't difficult to have Charlton share at length re his films... he never once asked what Patti and I were doing there. But the interesting and **sad** thing was what he said in the session to these heads of TV, radio and press... that **"the greatest contribution America has made to Bangladesh is the movie industry."** Having learned that there were literally **hundreds of porn shops** in Dacca... with **American flicks**... I knew immediately that, to true Muslims, this was such an offense. (I would allude to this 20 years later, in my 9/11/01 monthly letter, as one reason for Muslim dislike for the West… our immorality, both here and exported.)

* * * * * * * * * *

A group of young Bengalis told Patti of their need for **English**, so she laid out a plan for a school of English… it would require gov't permission, and we knew that would be difficult. Returning from a driving trip to Kamalganj, I had to cross a river on a small barge… only 4 cars. I got out of my car, and met one of the other men, who happened to be the closest friend of the **Minister of Education …** he said he would introduce me. (God certainly finds ingenious ways to encourage us.) Soon I was invited to the home of the Minister… and perhaps providentially I took Terril with me (he had grown up in **Nigeria**), and on the floor of the Minister was a lion rug… which he had picked up in **Nigeria.** After an hour of warm sharing of stories, the subject of the school was finally brought up, and in a five-minute discussion, he said "**of course**"… normally 18-24 months **done in one hour.**

3/84 Patti's school is an overwhelming success—100% growth with 50 students, and a long waiting list. She now has a staff of 6, including one American she had come, and training the Bengalis as teachers.

CHAPTER 13

THE ETHICS OF BRIBERY

Bribery is such a normal part of everyday activities in much of the Third World… so every Christian mission has to develop their own guidelines in response to that, as virtually nothing happens without some form of pay-off. I was part of a group in a discussion on this, and how it relates to each mission agency.

The illustration used was from an actual situation… a mission who had recently had a barge loaded with sacks of concrete, coming in for building a church. **All** *fees had been paid, but the man demanded more payment, and small boats were circling this barge, ready to help themselves. Time was of essence. With a mission committed to not paying bribes, and people having sacrificed in giving for this project, what should be done?*

So in a no-win situation, there are at least 3 options: 1) accede; 2) not accede—change the system, or 3) be a reluctant compromiser. There are 3 levels of bribery: 1) Bribery is payment to someone for what he should not do; 2) Protection, when I know that negative results will occur, so I pay to protect myself and rights; and 3) Extortion, the withholding of what is rightfully mine without a *payment. <u>Bukshees</u> is a <u>voluntary</u> payment for that which a person <u>should</u> do (what in the States we might call a 'tip.')*

Cash is not the only means of giving a bribe, as it could also be a gift, or a favor, or use of status or influence. Many considerations were discussed, including: honesty--Christian witness--financial--urgency--the condoning and perpetuation of an unjust system--relations with customs--residential status--Scripture--colleagues--and more.

Each of the above considerations was looked at, and given a scale of 1-10, plus or minus, both in general principles and also in this particular case, then added up to see the consequences of making a payment and of not making a payment. The strong opinion in this case was that urgency and financial were the overriding priorities—that in this case it was extortion, not a bribe.

Noted that Scripture primarily condemns the one <u>taking</u> a bribe. We will act <u>against</u> our conscience even when we choose the <u>lesser</u> evil—our conscience <u>ought</u> to be bothered. However, God is greater than our conscience, and so we choose that which seems most right at that point in light of all considerations.

CHAPTER 14

THE CHURCH IN BANGLADESH

I've always felt that a **Kingdom** agenda should be primary to institutional... in Chicago I had created the Chicago Network... in Portland helped initiate Evangelicals for Social Action. So now I'm in Bangladesh ... not as a missionary, but a relief and development person, and the question for me ... is there a Kingdom agenda beyond my present role?

I had met **Dr. Mina Malakar,** a medical doctor... a very astute lady... and in one of my times with her I asked: "What can HEED do to help **develop leadership** for the Church in Bangladesh?" To which she replied... **"What did you say?"...** and I repeated the question. Her response was so direct ... "That question has never been asked in the history of this country... if they did, the missionaries would have to go home." Then she went on to say "and some of them are here because they **can't make it at home**"... and then began to mention names. Knowing some of them, I felt she was right. (One missionary later said to me "I'm not sure where I'd go.")

I had been meeting occasionally with some of the leaders of various mission agencies, and began to conclude that the historic mission methodology was probably not going to be very effective in that country. From what I could understand, in over 100 years, there had been less than **150** Muslims converted. This of course is not unusual, as even **Samuel Zwemer**, considered the father of modern Muslim missions, may have had only half a dozen converts in his lifetime in the Middle East. To Muslims, becoming a Christian was to become a **Westerner.**

1/23 I am wrestling with the whole matter of what can be done to effectively relate the Gospel to the <u>Islamic world</u>. It seems as though the present church with its Hindu background may not be able to assimilate the Muslim convert—that is, without having them give up all of their tradition & culture. It seems that if God is going to do something in that culture it may look very different from the present Church... little or no singing... pray 5x a day... not change their names, etc... not call themselves Christians.

Dilip Dutta was the national head of the major Baptist mission group in the country, and we had a good relationship. Dilip asked me to be the opening speaker at an annual conference of pastors, and I asked him what he was looking for... what were the hopes of the Church? Having been influenced by western thinking about church growth, he said their goal was to have **100 new churches in 10 years.** I thought hmmmm... how do I approach this?

I asked Dilip if the church is like a family, and he agreed. So my question to him was... that in looking at **a church of believers as family 'A'**... and a group of **Muslims as family 'B'**... "how many family 'A's are there, which... when a person from family

'B' looks at family 'A', they say 'I like family 'A' better than my family… **I'm going to change families?**'" He said: "none." To which I responded "a healthy family produces healthy children… a sick family produces sick children… do you really want 100 new sick families? What if you had a 10 year goal of **10 healthy families!**" I had grown to believe that for a Muslim to respond to the Gospel, it really meant changing families.

7/30 Today Dilip called & came over—concerned re events via gov't, restrictions, teaching Arabic in schools, etc. Seemed heavy-hearted. I finally told him I'd say frankly & candidly what I felt:

- *that the mission groups were <u>reacting</u>, not planning*
- *reacting to a <u>shadow</u>, nothing concrete yet*
- *the point of discussion should not be the papers coming out of gov't, but what is the Gospel*
- *Acts 4—in persecution, they prayed "give us boldness"*
- *national leaders should get together and plan 5 years with <u>no</u> foreigners and <u>no</u> outside funding… $ is a temporary crutch*
- *it's obvious that virtually all the Christian leaders feel that foreigners should go home… that we tend to control, be paternalistic, stay here out of our own personal or institutional needs*
- *the Church here will probably not be united until we leave*
- *2 things divide the Church, power and $, and expats contribute to conflict through both*
- *it is not Asian to say a direct "<u>no</u>", so nationals are nodding their heads but saying 'no' inside when asked by westerners if we should stay*
- *I believe the Church could be united in less than 5 years if we all left.*

*I told Dilip those are the things I'd like to say to the national church leaders. He said I shouldn't, that they'd say "**he's a dangerous person.**" I asked why, & he said that they'd say: "**he knows us.**" He affirmed in spades everything I expressed... that he was so discouraged & fed up with the Christian leaders here, & wanted to quit the whole thing... I prayed with him.*

What a heavy thing—how to encourage and support the body of Christ here—who are they even? What is my role in that, as one who is not part of a mission, but as committed to God's body here?

In my efforts to turn HEED over to a full Bengali Board, many had initially said it wouldn't work, but by the time I left several mission groups asked me to come and tell them how to do it. The Australian Baptists were deeply committed to contextualized missions, and they asked me to speak at their annual conference... *spoke 8 times in 3 days. One of the men told me "how wonderful, you have given me a whole new perspective on my ministry." And one of the women told Patti, who had spoken twice, that her role would be that of helping mission wives discover their gifts."*

I think that God was using us in some small ways... in both the mission community and with the local church.

* * * * * * * * * *

A Bengali Soul Mate

I had grown to believe long ago that one's ministry is so much more effective when not being done alone. In Chicago and Portland I had those in my life who walked closely with me, at times via real accountability, but especially in encouragement, affirmation, and support in prayer, through both good and difficult times. So now where do I find that here in Bangladesh? Sadly, I did not find that in the expat or mission community... most didn't really understand the need for a relationship of depth or intimacy, one that is mutual... that embellishes life in every way. But in my second year, I met Ashish Bowl, a Bengali pastor who had a church on the outskirts of Dacca... a young man, full of energy, and deeply spiritual... not a part of the 'old guard.'

Wed. Apr 7 Sunday a.m. I stood up to preach at Gethsemane, & felt what I had on several occasions while preparing —'what am I doing this for, what do I have to say to these people?' How could I really communicate, even through an interpreter, anything of significance to an almost totally illiterate crowd. Felt totally inadequate, wanted to be immediately translated—right then and there, but then knew I had no recourse—I had to go on. As the pastor interpreted, at times he took twice as long to say what I had said... who knows, maybe he gave his own good Palm Sunday sermon. Anyway, it seemed to be received well, & today Ashish came to the office to say how much all the people said they were challenged by it. Our gardener & the Samonte's aya (Mele) had also said how much they had learned, as did Bithi, so I guess God used it— it had to be Him, as I felt so totally inadequate.

Ashish then expressed strongly his desire to have me preach again, & to be more involved with him ... that I've been involved in ministry for as long as he is old —that Westerners can't do the evangelizing, but that he would very much like the support & counsel & help & assistance I can give him. I believe he's one of the more open & honest ministers in the clergy here... has real integrity.

8/24 Ashish came by the office and we had a chat for a bit. Again he talked about my input for his ministry, that he was so challenged by the recent sermon I gave at his church, by the comments I made about not evangelizing but preaching Christ to his people, challenging them in Christian growth, so they can do the ministry. Said he preached this way last Sun. & results were amazing. Then we talked about Muslim evangelism, & I think of the young preachers he alone has the picture, to not have them change their name, etc. We had a good time of prayer for each other —I had told him before that I wanted him to be praying for me, that I need that from him.

As in most of the third world, there is a pecking order, a hierarchy of leadership, and it is important for the young to defer to age and seniority. *Most of the younger pastors had little respect for most of those older, and on one occasion I asked Ashish if they collectively couldn't move out together in new ways, but he simply said that they couldn't... had to wait for the older to die out. I had him come to our project up country in Kamalganj, and be the guest speaker for a week-end... he was powerful and effective.*

He and I began to meet every week for lunch, alternating each week... one week at his home and the next week at mine... so helpful to me in learning not only the culture, but the many nuances of the national church. (Bangladesh was **1/4th of 1% Christian,** mostly Catholic.) He was bright, energetic and fun... one of the few educated pastors.

During one of my bouts with **malaria**, Ashish heard about it while he was at a meeting... which he hurriedly left, and came over to our home. I was deathly ill, but glad to see him... and he got down on his knees by the side of the bed... took hold of my wrist... squeezing it so extremely tight, and then, lifting his other hand, went off in a prayer in Bengali that didn't seem to stop.

Ashish had a church that was flourishing, and some of his colleagues thought it was because I was giving him funds... which he knew wasn't true... it was common for missionaries to help provide funds for young pastors in their early ministry. The only time I ever gave Ashish anything was when I'd return from the States... once a pair of Levis, once a big jar of peanut-butter... as I never wanted to be in the position of sugar-daddy. And yet, his church was growing so well that he built a second floor on it, which would become their place of worship... and with **no chairs**, which is really how Bengalis live. For many the only places they used chairs was at church... a Western thing... they always sat on their haunches, or on the floor.

Ashish Bowl said tonite that 80% of his church is unemployed, and yet they are one of only two churches supporting a pastor in the Baptist denomination here. And he's hoping to add two interns soon. He really has a heart that cares, and it shows.

* * * * * * * * * *

To Stay, or Leave?

That was the question I asked the Lord in San Jose, and the answer came through loud and clear. Now we faced the same issue, as the Board had asked us to stay indefinitely. We had agreed to stay on one more year after our 3-year assignment, open to a longer period, but hopefully we would return to the States by the end of that year, 1984. And any extension would be determined after at least 2 months back in the States during the summer.

5/30 The last month has been one of exhaustion physically, mentally, emotionally, spiritually— including a week of the worst dysentery I've had since being here. But what an honor to have been asked by the largest Bengali church here to preach at the combined Easter services.

The weather has been devastating for the people here—ten days of constant rain, 12-15 inches in <u>one</u> day. Three people died in one day in the camp where our cleaning lady lives, and she and her household of eight sleep all night sitting up, with water ankle-deep in their 8x10 room.

The gov't has published a book on HEED's work in improving rice production. In addition, one of our engineers (from Holland) has made a significant contribution. A firm in London sent 3 prototype foot-powered lathes, one each to Asia (HEED), Africa, and S. America. Our man determined that it would not function properly, changed the design, and now the London firm has declared the original obsolete, and the gov't here may have it produced on a large scale.

August/'84 Leaving Bangladesh 6 weeks ago was both easy and difficult... I felt joy and relief, but also a tremendous sense of sadness. For the last 2 years our mission has been very shorthanded and the added work load, along with the normal struggles of getting things done there, had brought me to a point of physical, mental, emotional and spiritual exhaustion I've never experienced before.

In fact, I was scheduled to leave 2 weeks later, but 3 weeks earlier I had recalled the old principle that work expands to fill the time given for it, and concluded that we could get 5 weeks of work done in 3 if we really worked at it, which would get me out of there earlier as well as add 2 extra weeks for the r & r back here in the States before at least 7 more months there. I <u>had</u> to get away — and Patti had already left 3 weeks earlier.

So with mixed emotions I left… relieved in getting away from the excessive work load that had just about crushed me, as well as the oppressive heat and rain. Almost 50% of the country was under water from some of the worst floods in history, and word I receive now is that maybe 2/3 of the country is under water… the world's largest delta is almost completely inundated. But also I was leaving a people and friends who would be struggling for their very lives, people I have grown to love deeply, where the average family spends 20% of their day just collecting firewood for home fuel, & most all efforts all day for everyone is given to simply exist. It was not an opportune time to leave, with valid reasons to both stay and leave. Which was right?

Three years ago we decided to go abroad for a brief period to expose ourselves as to how the majority of the world thinks and lives, for our own learning and growth. What an education this has been, but we have to leave soon, or stay many more years, as a number of our leading expats would be heading home in a year or two, and it wouldn't be good to have a new Director come at the same time some new replacements would be coming. Obviously it would be best to not have another change in leadership now.

I arrived back in Dacca Sept. 30, and told the Board I would give an answer within one week on whether or not we would stay on after April. Then while on a trip up-country, as I was musing on 'to stay or leave', the thought came to me from something in a business magazine years before... if you're the head of an organization, how do you determine priorities. And one statement was that the first thing to ask one's self would be **"what can only I do?"...** then delegate. And immediately I had the answer, as the thought of 'what can only I do' raced through my mind... **"be a grandfather to my grandkids...** we're going home." It was almost a no-brainer, and I informed the Board of my decision to not stay beyond April 1985.

* * * * * * * * * * *

The Last Days

I've said at times that our 4 years in Bangladesh were the **hardest... most difficult...** most **challenging** ... most **wonderful...** most **fulfilling...** most **rewarding** years of our lives. I was invariably over my head, but God's grace was experienced so strongly, and I believe we were able to accomplish some things that we had never dreamed of.

Our work has been received well by the gov't, and they recently published a book on our rice research and production... from our hospital our leprosy staff are treating over 1300 leprosy patients... we are heavily involved in the training of village health workers... we have trained many hundreds of people in handicrafts... changing from primarily curative to exclusively preventive medical care, and against all odds politically, we had reduced the infant mortality rate in one large area by 30% in 1 year. We have seen a bit of a response to the Good News.

We had set up a **scholarship fund**, helping more than 100 Christian young people continue their education. I felt that we had made a Kingdom contribution, and had done what was asked, to get HEED stabilized. But especially, HEED would now be **owned and run by Bengalis**... one English missionary/statesman said it was the largest turnover of a Christian mission in history. I had laid the groundwork... and we had developed **five-year goals for 47 program** areas... it would go well.

Before we left I made one last trip to each of our projects... *left Dacope with a real lump in my throat, though didn't feel the same at Kamalganj.* The Board had a lovely going-away evening for us, and I gave my **farewell speech all in Bangla**, during which time the power went out in the building, and I finished it by candlelight. They loved it.

So the question... what next? During the holiday season I had gone back to the States to look at three or four opportunities that had arisen. Of several possibilities, the one at **Bethany Presbyterian Church** seemed the best fit at that time... we knew we'd need a place where we'd have emotional and spiritual support, coming from where we had had little... where our gifts would be a good match. And the job description seemed just right, **Director of Nurture & Outreach**... plus, that is where **Pete and Linda** attended. So while in Seattle we looked at houses, bought, and later scheduled a departure date, my birthday, **April 16**.

On the way we stopped over in **Hong Kong** to be with Mick and Kay Marshall, missionaries from Bethany. During our time there we went with them into China, **smuggling Bibles** inside luggage. Each of us had two duffle bags, with clothes on top, and when we arrived at a major hotel, we went into the restroom... put all the Bibles in one bag and our clothes in the other. (When I came out of the stall, there stood **2 Red Guards**, but nothing said.) Then the bags of Bibles would be left in a hotel compartment, and the receipt would be given to a local Christian, who would later pick up the bags.

Walking the narrow streets, a man invited Patti and me into his 'home'... told us of his family in San Francisco, and I suggested that he write a letter, which we could mail back in the States. We mailed the letter... make phone contact... and the next year, when we were in S.F., we met them, and they had a huge Chinese luncheon for us. Fun time.

CHAPTER 15

IMPRESSIONS FROM BANGLADESH

When I suggested to Patti (1980) that we go to a Third World country "to get an education"... I never dreamed the extent to which that would be true. From being in a culture not too unlike that of Jesus' day, it was indeed a wonderful eye-opener as to how much of the world operates ... so different from our Western world. The following are some of what I felt I learned from those 4 years... mostly from my journals.

1. *Relief vs Development:* **Relief**... *immediate need, give a fish, Jesus when healing* **Development**... *long-range, self-sufficiency, teach how to fish, Jesus training the 12*

2. *Jesus life was lived out* **contrary to cultural norms**... *far more of a radical/revolutionary than I had ever imagined... upset the establishment... against most every tradition and custom*

3. *The **Gospel is irrational**, absurd... to save life, lose it... humble self to be exalted... love your enemy... turn the cheek... creation from 0... God's purposes not via the wise*

4. *Awareness of the supernatural and spiritual powers of darkness*

5. *Love is **an act of the will**, not an emotion... most S. Asian marriages are arranged by the parents, so Paul says "husbands love your wives"... we 'fall in love' while they learn to love as an act of the will*

6. *Can't be done effectively alone... a dart--small dent... a spear---deep penetration, from weight of shaft... Paul never went alone*

7. *Risks/Rewards... life as God intends it is meant to involve **challenge, and risk**, and sacrifice... which is at the heart of personal growth... less in tangible rewards but far more in personal satisfaction*

8. *The tendency to interpret life from my own cultural heritage or context, not from a biblical perspective... more committed to a social/economic/political aspect of life than Kingdom of God... more controlled by my culture than by the Church and God's people. How did that happen? Christianity came into an eastern world... (now, seeing Scripture from an eastern perspective, it becomes a different book.) But Christian **theology** was developed through Greek thought... so the Gospel came to be translated in theological terms, and Eastern theologians say "your minds have been converted, but not your hearts."*

9. *Life is lived far more around family and group... we more individual*

10. *Evangelism vs Social Concern — inextricably linked. "The words interpret the deeds, and the deeds validate the words"... Leslie Newbigen. Not an either/or, but both/and... come together in* **compassion**

11. *The amazing joy in many Christians, in spite of deep poverty and discrimination*

12. *Most things are far more gray than black and white*

13. *As C.S. Lewis says: "When one has been to another world, they see everything differently"*

14. *The beautiful gift to us in seeing the beauty in those with so little, and who loved us*

U. S. Ministries

CHAPTER 16

PASTOR BUD

Bethany was considered the '**charismatic**' of the Presbyterian churches in the Seattle area... a church of about 300. My position included missions, deacon oversight, home groups, college age and evangelism/ outreach. **Dick Denham** had been pastor there for more than 20 years... had a warm and inviting spirit, and the worship was a combination of traditional and contemporary... both Patti and I really enjoyed the warmth of worship there.

However, administration was not one of Dick's gifts, and after a few months he asked if I would assume that responsibility. One day at a staff meeting it was mentioned that there were **8** visitors that Sunday, and Wendy, the church secretary, simply said that was quite normal. I remember thinking... normal ??? That's maybe **400 visitors a year**, with the same attendance for years. So I asked 2 of our women to head up a Newcomers Committee, and they developed an effective procedure for being in touch with visitors... studies had shown that if a visitor is contacted by a **lay** person within 36 hours, there is an 85% chance that they will return.

I moved ahead in initiating a number of things, but ran into an unexpected wall. At the first meeting of the new admin committee of Elders, I suggested how we might proceed, but was told by one of the Elders… **"you don't lead, you're an employee"…** now where do I go with this. I saw that I had to be discreet in how we would get things done, but was able to move a number of things ahead. When I arrived they had **50** people in 'home groups', and 15 months later we had **185**.

I had done some homework on our finances… discovering we had **9** different bank accounts… in several different banks… one with **$20,000** drawing **no interest** which nobody knew about. I asked **Dan Baumgartner**, a businessman, to head up the finance committee, and they really got our finances in shape. (He later felt a call to the ministry, went to seminary, and became the senior pastor at Bethany, providing great leadership.) Patti initiated a **healing/prayer ministry**, with about a dozen of us meeting every Sunday evening for a year, under her tutelage… and some wonderful things began to happen in healings… still a significant ministry there.

One ministry I learned of was via Jerry Kirk, one of my close YL colleagues in earlier days: the **Lay Pastor ministry.** He now had a huge church in Cincinnati, with **75** Lay Pastors… a ministry in which a lay person is trained to actually **pastor a 'flock' of 6 or 7 families**… be in such close touch and care for them, that when a family member got ill, or had some other need, they didn't call the church, but their Lay Pastor. I took one of our Elders with me to see what they were doing in Cincinnati… we were overwhelmed, and decided to establish that at Bethany… then trained a number of people for this.

I would preach on occasion, one of which was a communion Sunday. In the church basement I had seen a **railing**... not used for years... so for that Sunday I **placed it between the pulpit and the lectern**... had decided I would preach on the healing nature of the bread and wine, including the story of my having been healed at a communion service. Also, one of the participants in the healing/prayer ministry had had a miraculous healing. She was going in for major surgery... removal of a tumor the size of a grapefruit... but someone told her that she should first go to the Elders of her church (Japanese Presbyterian), and ask them to pray for her, which she did. The pastor brought a number of Elders together, and said: "we're not used to this, but **Scripture says to do it"...** so they did... and when she went in for an examination prior to the operation, the **tumor was gone.**

So as part of the sermon I had her come up and relate her story... then I shared mine as well. At the end of the service, I invited the people to come forward for communion... to kneel at the railing... and Elders would serve the elements... and, after partaking, if any would like prayer, that Elders and the prayer team would be there to pray with/for them. At each of the two services there were 20-25 who sought prayer... it was a powerful time.

Although I believe God used us at Bethany, there were many times when I felt discouraged, just feeling I was not being able to move things ahead. Toward the end of my second year, staff associate **Linda** was taking me to the airport, and I told her that when I returned a week later I was going to resign... but when I got back, **she** had resigned... **drat.**

Dick had been on **dialysis for 30+ years**, one of the longest in all the U.S… and he was awaiting a kidney transplant. So now with reduced staff the timing would not be appropriate to resign. Some months later Dick received his kidney transplant, so it was good I was there through the months of his recovery. But even with Dick's beautiful spirit, and a real heart for people, I still felt I had to resign… feeling that God must have something else for me. But what? So Patti and I prayed about this, and on **February 1,** I resigned, giving 5 months notice… which would be exactly four years from the day I started.

While I felt I needed to make a change in terms of career, in many ways it was not easy, as we had developed many close friendships there… and even now, many years later, still enjoy close ties to some. Dick and I remained close friends, even through the years after he resigned, which he had done shortly after my time there. We stayed on at the church, and after I had begun a new career, working out of my home, the interim pastor asked me to come back and have my office there, to handle the many requests for weddings… many outsiders liked the old Gothic architecture of the church, and wanted to get married there.

That was an enjoyable opportunity, as many couples came who had little church background, and it was an occasion to help them discover… as I would say… that their marriage would work better with **Jesus… the glue of all creation… and of marriage… t**han without him. After hearing each family background, I would tell them "I'm going to take 5-7 minutes and talk about the Christian faith"… on occasion hearing a response like "I've never heard it like that before"… or, "that's what we've been looking for." Our years in YL had helped us understand how to communicate the Gospel clearly to non-believers... and some even joined the church. (Over the years I performed 50-60 weddings, and so far as I know, to date just 2 divorces. My minor in Counseling in graduate studies was of great help... and a personality profile questionnaire I used would indicate areas of health and/or potential problems. In some cases it was obvious that professional counseling would be necessary... I would not continue if they did not pursue that. And in **every case** where that person went into counseling the couple broke up.) Bethany still holds a special place in our hearts... a marvelous ministry to the community... and we look back at the Bethany years of 1985-1989 with many fond memories.

CHAPTER 17

THE TEETER TOTTER

I had six months or more to decide/discern what was ahead for me… much too early to consider retirement… (couldn't retire anyway… had never had a pension… except YL, and when we left I took the pension funds and blew them on dinner and a movie.) A group of us had been meeting that spring, looking at ways to carry out a **vision for a city**… coming from some meetings that Ray Bakke had in Seattle earlier. So he and my good Chicago friend Bill Leslie were encouraging me to start a **Leadership Foundation** … whatever that was. Then YL asked if I would come back and head up **YL in Asia**… I thought that could be fun and a great challenge.

Sometime in June I read something of Bruce Larson's, in which he stated, essentially, **"do the hard thing."** So which way do I go? I knew YL well… conversely, I didn't even know what a Leadership Foundation (LF) was… I was relatively new to Seattle… and really knew few people there. So narrowing it to those 2 options, it was back to the question, "Lord, what do you have ahead for me?" and, to the pro and con routine:

	Pro	**Con**
Young Life	*Years of experience*	*Raise own support*
	Many good friends & colleagues	*Present top leadership questionable*
	Remain in int'l work/Asia	*What's the future for int'l*
	Some good people, with vision	*Primarily youth… limiting?*
	Provides structure and accountability	

	Pro	**Con**
Leadership Foundation	*Need for Kingdom ministry in Seattle*	*Who shares the same vision?*
	Encouraged by misc. people	*What **is** the vision?*
	Network developing nationally	*No present structure/ accountability*
	Use of my gifts of strategy/ creativity	*Where nurtured?*
	Place for risk and newness	*Ego?*
	Pastor to some now 'alone'	*Funding*

Patti and I also made a list of all the moves we had made, going back to 1951 when we went to Philadelphia… how had God led… what had been accomplished in each… what gifts were used… what was fulfilling/rewarding… what was hard/ difficult… what lessons were learned… and more.

God gave me a tremendous peace about the future, and I was really free of any apprehension or anxiety. II Chronicles 20 was a strong confirmation of that—King Jehoshaphat asks God if he should go to battle against 3 armies attacking them… God says yes, but "you *won't have to fight—I will fight for you." King J sends his armies out, with the <u>choir</u> in front. The moment the choir started singing, the 3 enemy armies started fighting each other, and 100% wiped each other out. Then J. was "quiet and at peace and rest." The Lord simply seemed to be saying to me—I will take care of you—just praise me, and you will have true peace of mind. And I really felt that. What's important isn't what I do, but His honor.*

After finishing Chronicles and Ezra, I was going to skip Nehemiah, since I had gone over that 6 mos. ago with some tapes. But I thought, no, there's always more to learn. Well—ch. 1… in Nehemiah's strong desire for the wall to be rebuilt, I saw me and Seattle. Then in ch. 2 he asks the king for letters of permission and for materials from other kings of other countries, and I saw the need for resources and relationships for a Seattle ministry. Is God asking me to do this Foundation thing? I see me in every page—is that God or me?

Getting into the book of Esther, the one part that jumped out at me – "God has brought you here for just such a time as this." Am I arrogant to think that God is bringing <u>me</u> to minister significantly to Seattle at this time? If that is so, how humbling and how very much I will need prayer and boldness and encouragement and strength and insight—it must be God's, not mine. I do not feel at all adequate for the task, but within my sense of inadequacy, I realize the need for empowerment, that "I can do all things through Christ who strengthens me." And "by my God have I leaped over a wall." If something extraordinary happens, it will be done not by ordinary means—it will be the power of the Holy Spirit.

In our Chicago years, we had come to know **Sister Anne**, a director at **The Cenacle**, a Catholic Order providing retreat centers and spiritual direction. Patti especially had gone there a number of times for silent retreats, and we had seen unusual spiritual insight from her... I had her come once to speak to a group of college kids, and she talked on '**the use of Scripture in prayer**'... powerful. Now Sister Anne was at The Cenacle in **Vancouver, B.C.,** so the two of us decided that we would go up there for several days of retreat, to see what we might hear from God as to whatever was in **His** mind for us. On arrival we met with her for an hour each, and she gave me several pamphlets to read, but just one Scripture verse... **Isaiah 43:18-19.**

After dinner the evening of the second day, I went for a long walk, and on return...

I sat down in the gazebo by the rose garden, and there sat a Bible. Opening it to Isaiah 43, I looked at vs 18 and 19, and lo and behold, those 2 verses were <u>marked</u>. I looked quickly through the entire Bible to look for other markings, but there were none that I could find. That Scripture said: **"let go of the past—I'm going to do <u>something new</u>."** *O God, lead me.*

During July and August I was meeting with a variety of people, some of whom wanted to get me involved in their 'thing', and I felt caught in a swirl... feeling pulled in a lot of directions. But two of the more promising meetings were with George Kovats of Stewardship Foundation, and with John Woodyard of the huge Murdock Trust... both liked the Leadership Foundation (LF) idea... and it just seemed so right... so I felt that was what I should do. So now it was the process of establishing a new non-profit... we would call it the **Northwest Leadership Foundation...** (NLF), officially formed September 15, 1989.

* * * * * * * * * *

The New Beginnings

Reid Carpenter, former YL colleague, had initiated the first Leadership Foundation (LF) in Pittsburgh, and now the half a dozen or more met annually to share vision and mutual concerns. Their next meeting would be in late September, so I would go to that and see what I could learn about this new venture.

Sept. 27 A good time in Pittsburgh. Wow! They have so much going for them—amazing. It was good input and exposure. But Mon. I was feeling lower than a snake's hips—feeling inadequate, uncertain, and generally wishing I were heading for something else. Will we be funded? Will what I'd be doing make any difference? Will I <u>fail?</u> Is it too late to bail out? Wished there would be something come that would be a challenge <u>and</u> give security. This feels so alone and uncertain… but I need to constantly be reminded of what God gave me—Isaiah 43:18 & 19, and Phil 3:13, to let go of the past, and trust that a whole new thing is what God has for me.

Sept. 29 Yesterday Patti and I prayed for each other before she headed off for her day and I for mine. What a good day I had, it really was an encouraging day. Thank you Lord! How much I realize that if God does something significant through me, it will be <u>Him</u> and <u>not Bud.</u> Lord, prepare my heart, and go before— preparing the way for what <u>you</u> want to see happen. I've been going through Mark, and first Jesus was empowered by the Spirit, then called several men to himself… then broke several traditions, i.e. eating with sinners… Lord Jesus, may I be empowered and invaded by your Spirit… be given that small cadre of men with whom to minister… not be afraid to be non-traditional… and then minister strongly in your name. So be it. amen.

But I felt like a mosquito at the nudist colony… where do I begin? I knew little about what a LF was… each was different in form… and at times I thought to myself… **what in the world have I gotten myself** into… this is way beyond me. What I think I realized ultimately was that to really effect Christ being seen in the city, one had to take on a totally different paradigm of ministry… that of **loving the city… serving the city…** that **words** don't bear witness to the power of the Gospel. (When the Billy Graham Crusade in Seattle asked me to head up their Love In Action Committee, they readily acknowledged that their crusades have relatively little impact with urban people… the blue-collar, the less-advantaged.)

I sensed a basic LF concept was to provide **Kingdom thinking** and **compassion** for the **hurting people of the city**… and how to help the Church develop ministry to those. So I began to interview leaders of ministries in/to the city… would ask them their mission… goals… strengths… needs … limitations… successes… lessons learned… budgets… who else was doing something similar and how different from them… connect with them in any way… future dreams/plans… and more.

After visiting **50-60** directors of agencies and ministries, I began to see who were **institutional** people, and who were **Kingdom** people (unfortunately, too many of the former)… who was making it happen, and who was doing it with mirrors. And I was really learning the city… someone said after that first year that I probably knew more than any other person in the city as to who was doing what, and to what effect. Then I began to get requests for assistance of various sorts… program evaluation… organizational review… vision clarification, etc., and I sensed that my role might be that of a catalyst... helping others succeed.

One of the things I did early on was to begin meeting weekly for prayer with several black pastors, one of whom had his church running the **Holly Park Day Care Center...** in **the largest public housing project in the city.** It became apparent that it was not only being run poorly, but... the church didn't really want it... it was losing money... and they **owed the IRS and the County almost $20,000.** I paid for two studies as to its profitability... both positive... so I helped develop a new Board... raised funds for operations and debt reduction... then got ECOM to take it over. A few years later it was considered a **national model.**

Harvey Drake had founded Emerald City Outreach Ministries **(ECOM),** and we became good friends. They had a tutoring program of **15 kids**, and since Patti had real expertise in this area, I suggested the possibility of having her assist them. By the end of the year there were **50** kids being tutored twice a week, with **50** volunteers. Then I suggested to Harvey that while this was so good, it was not connecting those kids with **their roots, the black church**... let's put this in black churches. So NLF created **Tutor's LInc...** and that first year we were in 7 black churches... the next year in **13.** Patti had a major role in writing a tutor-training manual... published by Washington Mutual... and the next year NLF ran the tutor training for all the major agencies in the city involved in tutoring... CAYA, Catholic Community Services, and others.

We were asked by Operation Blessing (CBN/700 Club) to become their vehicle for disbursing matching funds and material goods for emergency and special needs of the poor… ultimately would end up **disbursing almost $2 million** through many churches and agencies… also influenced their procedures nationally for fund distribution… moving from cash distribution to store vouchers.

Long before **World Vision** (WV) moved north, they asked us to help set up their ministry locally, so I put together a **blue-ribbon Board** of civic and business leaders… then we hired a person to set up and run tutoring programs, and handed Tutor's LInc over to them. Also, WV didn't want to have the local person on their payroll from a distance (So. Cal.), so for several years NLF had WV personnel on our payroll… their staff in **Seattle, Tacoma, Houston** and **Detroit**… funded of course by WV. In a separate program, utilizing funds from WV, we created a **job-development training** program in 4 churches, with hundreds of unemployed getting jobs. Then some years later, when WV moved to Federal Way, we entered into a mutual agreement in which they would do all their ministry in the Seattle-Tacoma area in collaboration with NLF.

When I first began NLF someone suggested that I call **Dick Crowe**… which I did… and after trying to figure out who and why, our mutual YL interests clicked, and he said he'd like to have me meet a couple of African-American brothers from Tacoma. At a restaurant, and after about 20 minutes of general chit-chat… out of the blue one of the two said: "**you scare us… you know us too well.**" I really didn't even know what we were talking about that made him think that, but I know there was freedom in our conversation. I became close friends of both, and helped develop their respective outreaches in their churches. Over a period of several years we participated in planning and programs for the **Hilltop** area, including heading up some long-range planning days. I met with the **Tacoma Ministerial Alliance**, the group of black pastors who met regularly… then in 1993 **Ron Detrick** joined us on staff there in Tacoma.

Habitat for Humanity asked if I would assist in helping to develop their operations with black churches. I had been meeting with several black pastors for a couple of years, and so told Habitat that those churches would probably select their own families, but Habitat insisted "no", **their family selection committee** would do that. So I suggested that we meet with these pastors… who confirmed strongly what I had said… that they, the church, would select the family. That was the beginning of my **meeting every week for 6 years with 6 key black pastors.**

About the second year of our weekly time together, I mentioned that we had an interest-free loan available to us for housing… via the Memphis LF… and one of the men said **"Bud, tell us how to do it"**… and I said "we'll create the **Coalition for Community Renewal."** Later, I drove to Olympia to make sure we had the non-profit organization set up before the next day, when NLF was the co-sponsor of a half-day on development, featuring **Jack Kemp**… now we had something tangible to present as a vehicle for community change.

We got into housing… several single homes… bought 2 duplexes… 3 acres for 20 homes… and pursued a variety of other programs… so much seemed to be happening that **Howard Schultz,** owner of **Starbucks**, gave us a franchise. Then he took it back… said everyone else would want one… but CCR would be the recipient of the proceeds of the Starbucks in the **'hood'**, and that would go to Zion Prep Academy, headed up by **Doug Wheeler,** in whose office we met every week.

Over a period of time suburban pastors began to meet with us, primarily under the influence of **Aaron Haskins**, who was working with PromiseKeepers... and what developed was an amazing time of reconciliation and relationships of **urban/ suburban, black/anglo**. That even included one session of foot-washing... taking off our shoes and socks, and washing each other's feet.

Over the years the weekly meeting with the 6 men continued, but CCR would host a monthly meeting for the larger group... ultimately a beautiful catalyst for a meeting of 40-50 pastors and ministry leaders of all denominations and color. The group was influential enough, that in making an **appeal for clemency** to the Governor to not deport one of the Hispanic pastors, who had sexually abused a person prior to his conversion... and where appropriate amends had been made... that **the only pardon given by the Governor in 4 years** was to this pastor... one of the CCR men... and the official letter was read at the last meeting I attended prior to moving to Portland.

* * * * * * * * * *

At one of our weekly CCR meetings, I said to Tony, pastor of a large church... "Tony, I tell people that the black culture is more similar to **Bangladesh** culture then to our **A**nglo culture", and he said: "of course, **we're third world.**" And I responded... "I know it, and **you're more biblical than we are.**" "How's that?" "Well, Scripture says 'as a man **thinks in his heart, so is he'...** and 'my son, **keep your heart** with all diligence, for

out of it are the issues of life.' We think here (pointing to my head), and you think here (pointing to my heart)."

From our years in Bangladesh, I think one of the gifts God gave Patti and me in living in that culture was to understand how people think and live differently within different cultures, and the privilege in perhaps becoming genuinely bi-cultural... seeing almost everything through two different lenses. Doug Wheeler enjoyed calling me **"boy"**... said it was his way of saying I was a '**brother.**'

One of the challenging groups I was meeting with was a group of Christian attorneys... met monthly for a year or two, looking at issues of biblical justice, and how that relates to our cities today. Ray Bakke had pointed out that there are over **1000 verses in the Bible on the poor**, and **67** on **justice for the poor and oppressed**... I realized that I had never heard one sermon on any of those. So one of the things I did was to set up a series of meetings in 6 black churches, with black and white Christian **judges and attorneys**... to have open forums on areas such as tenant/landlord issues, etc. It was a winner.

* * * * * * * * * *

During the years I had come to the conclusion that the suburban church needed the city more than the city needed them... needed the city **for their own salvation.** For decades the debate has gone on as to evangelism vs social action... an inappropriate term for ministering in Jesus' name. '**Witness**' is usually seen as **verbal** declaration of the Gospel, but in the Greek that word is '**martyr**'... used about 20 times in the book of Acts, and **never verbal**... "You will be my **exhibit A,** in Jerusalem, Judea... ."

(Acts 1:8)… i.e., 'wherever you go in the world, when people see you, **they will see Me**.'

One group had come asking for assistance in their ministry, subtitled "The Church united to **take** the city." I suggested to them "how about the Church united to **love** the city, to **serve** the city." So in the monthly letters I wrote, it was often a biblical perspective on the Church and the city… and some of those letters are included in the Appendix.

* * * * * * * * * *

NLF had grown to where we now had staff in **Seattle, Tacoma and Spokane**, and for several years I had wanted to pass on the baton… felt I had run enough organizational stuff in my life, and would be happy to hand over all the administrivia. On two successive years I had taken someone with me to the annual meetings of Foundation leaders, hoping that one was the right person to take over… but finally, when **Dave Hillis** came on board in Tacoma, I knew the right person was there.

So in 1997 I created **Northwest Leadership Associates** (NLA), and we laid out a plan where I would assist NLF in any way that I could… virtually like a subsidiary, including helping with the oversight and development of staff in Seattle.

A few years later, when we were moving from Seattle to Portland in 2004, my new Board of NLA asked me to give a summary report of **NLF/NLA** to date. That report is provided in the Appendix.

CHAPTER 18

EXPANDING OPPORTUNITIES

Being free of organizational responsibilities allowed me greater latitude in responding to various opportunities... some of which had to do with persons or groups wanting to start a **non-profit ministry.** I ended up helping to start about a dozen new ones, but helped that many or more to not start... some individuals had unrealistic dreams... or too much caffeine... or whatever. One pastor from Everett called, and then came down to discuss his dream. While I would never tell a person they shouldn't start one, I tried to make sure they were asking all the right questions... and a week later I received a letter from that pastor, saying: "thanks for telling me what I didn't want to hear."

For about 9 years Seattle Pacific University provided free office space for us on campus. (That was fortunate, since we operated on a fairly bare-bones budget... in 1994 the NLF budget was **$80,000,** but we had more than **$1.3 million** go through our books... as with other LFs, it seemed easier to raise funds for others than for ourselves.) I was assisting SPU as to urban ministry opportunities, and in working with pastors from black churches. We set up a program in which the college would provide 3/1 matching funds for a student who enrolled from their church... and I arranged for a **scholarship program** for minority students. Also, I had encouraged them to incorporate Ray Bakke in their programs, and we were able to have him become an adjunct prof... from Chicago.

One model for urban ministry was Bill Leslie's church in Chicago, LaSalle Street Church, to which I've alluded earlier. One day I received a call from a **denomination** as to their wanting to start a new church in the city... the Church Growth movement was seen largely in terms of planting new churches. So I met with them... listened for an hour, and then asked a number of questions... will the new church be an **ethnic** church? (knowing they already had 4 or 5 such)... or a **geographical** area in the city?... or... do you want to initiate a **ministry to** the city. (Some urban experts encourage the theory that it's often better to first initiate a **mission**... which will **later** become a church.)

They were intrigued with the idea, and I suggested a procedure that would first involve all their suburban churches... and then, create a non-profit. I told them it would cost a couple bucks for me to do this for them, but that I'd raise x times that. But they said the denomination would only provide funds for a '**new church** plant.' So I called the **President** of the denomination, and he agreed to have breakfast. I flew to his city, explained the whole concept, and came home with a **check for $10,000...** so developed The **Urban Mission Alliance.**

UMA grew... and then I pointed out Nehemiah 11:1, where, after the walls of Jerusalem were rebuilt (of course it was still a place of devastation… who would want to go there?), God asked for **a tithe of people** to move into the city… (the church's **social tithe** to the city?). A few years later **6 or 7 families** moved from the suburbs into the city, to be part of UMA, developing effective ministry in/to/for the city… **and**, a new church began.

* * * * * * * * * *

Apples and Children

One new opportunity I enjoyed was not urban… very rural… however, having to do with the under-privileged. I had heard of **Ralph Broetje**… an **apple-grower** in southeast Washington. Ralph had **6000 acres**… the largest apple operation in the country… and had built **100+ homes for his workers.** And, he had built **a processing plant**… so had almost **1000 employees**. Being so remote, his (mostly Hispanic) workers were trucked in, or drove some distance, so initially he had built a **day-care center** where women could bring their children. Then he built the **homes**… and a **store**, and a **gas station**… and a **gymnasium** … and a **chapel**. An incredible community had developed, out in the middle of nowhere … kids went 17 miles to school.

I grew to know Ralph, and because of my interest in helping the under-class develop their own future, I mentioned to him one day the idea of selling the homes to his people, so they could build equity. He was intrigued with that, and I contacted a friend… Ph.D. in Urban Development… paid him $15 an hour to develop a plan for people to buy the home while Ralph still owned the land.

Then sometime later I talked with Ralph about having them **buy part of the business**... start with a **tithe... 600 acres**. (The well-known adage "give a man a fish, he'll eat for a day... teach him how to fish, and he'll eat the rest of his life"... but then the question is raised, '**but who owns the pond?**') He seemed intrigued with the idea, and I suggested that he find 6-10 of his key men who would want to do this, then set up an escrow account into which each would put perhaps $100 a month for 3 years, which would then be enough for a down payment. During that time he would teach them **business management, horticulture,** etc., so they would be equipped to handle their own operation.

A short while later he called and suggested the thought of doing this with the **10,000 acres** next door that were for sale... "are you with me on this, Bud?" Of course. Then... about 2 weeks later... he called, and said: **"Bud, I'm going to sell everything...** "and he was dead serious... spoke of so many family difficulties he was facing. I told him "I'll be down tomorrow."

I had been reading some of **Frederick Buechner's** writings on vocation... so provocative. He writes of how God puts into each person certain gifts, skills, talents... which, when lived out in one's life, become a **Kingdom gift** to the world. I sat in the living room with Ralph and his wife, Cheryl, and he talked about their concerns. I listened, and then said to Ralph: "unless I'm mistaken, aside from Jesus and your family, **Ralph Broetje has 2 loves... trees and children"...** and they both nodded. Then I said: "if Ralph Broetje gave up trees, **would part of Ralph die**, and the Kingdom would be decimated... what if you handed operations over to Robert, and you can focus more on children."

It wasn't long before they developed a large area of their acreage into an absolutely beautiful school, a high **school for problem kids**... drop outs... or those who just weren't making it... kids from all over the country, including several from Chicago's Cabrini-Green... **60 boys** in a first-class setting. And a couple of years ago they played for the state championship in 8-man football. Then they developed an elementary school... about **95 children.**

But perhaps the most amazing thing about Ralph is what he did for his **women employees**, as half of them had to work an **evening shift** in the processing plant... and Ralph began to feel that it just wasn't right for women to not be home in the evening with their family. So, he spent **$10 million** to develop a second processing plant, just so mothers could be at home in the evening. This is a family committed to living on 1% of their earnings... the rest is given away.

* * * * * * * * * * *

Albania

It was 1999, and there was the apparent 'ethnic cleansing' being carried out in Yugoslavia by **Milosevich** ... so almost a million **ethnic Albanians** fled from **Kosovo** to Albania. I got a call one day — **"Bud, can you go to Albania in 3 days"**... (sorta like 'can you go to Dacca in 2 hours.') So off I went, to assist the churches in Albania in their caring for the Kosovo refugees... the situation was too volatile for Patti to go with me.

Albania had previously been the most isolated country in the world... they had become Communist, and after the changes in Russia, and cutting themselves off from contact with China, they had virtually **0** communication with any country. In 1991 there was a revolution, and modest changes were made, although even today it is considered perhaps the most corrupt country in the world… (and from the 30+ countries I've been too, that may be fairly true.)

So far as we know, there were only 2 Christians in the country in 1991… but with the country now more open, soon various groups came in… including Billy Graham, and by 1999 there were probably **6-7000** believers. The different mission groups had formed a partnership in which they would work together (**AEP),** and when the refugee crisis hit they formed the **Albania Crisis Center** (ACC).

Yugoslavia was mostly Serbs, but many Albanians, mostly Muslims, had migrated to Kosovo, and lived there for years… so suddenly there were almost **800,000 Kosovo refugees** in Albania. AEP had set up a procedure for receiving goods coming in by both ship and truck… (although soon the trucking was stopped, since almost all were stopped and taken over by robbers.) But they would distribute these goods to churches around the country, and my task was to help coordinate and expedite much of this. The amazing thing was, that with Christians being far **1/5**[th] **of 1%** in the country, they were caring for almost **15%** of the refugees, and were feeling taxed and overwhelmed … but showing incredible compassion and caring. Some of them had as many as **10-12 living with them** in their small homes.

I was working with **Ina,** a deeply committed and passionate Christian woman… very bright… the woman selected by the government to meet with **Koffi Annan** when he came to Albania during the days I was there. An English mission had also sent a person to assist, so the 3 of us would meet to strategize… to which cities we would go, and how we to provide encouragement and assistance… so that rather than each church in a city making a request for goods from AEP in Tirana (the capitol), they would make one coordinated request. We would be meeting with all the pastors in each city.

The pastors were a tired, sometimes rather discouraged group, so I usually waited until we had taken care of organizational stuff, and then would wind up our time… telling them the story of **Onesimus**… a run-away slave, **immigrant** from Asia, who ran into **Paul** in Rome. He is converted, and Paul sends him back to **Philemon**, his 'owner'… knowing that almost always the slave would be killed… or, be branded, with **'Fugitive'** on his forehead the rest of his life. But in this case, and at Paul's behest, Philemon takes him back, and the first house church has begun in which **both slave and owner** are members.

Then I would relate the end of the story… about the **Church in Ephesus**… the most **major** church, in a **major** city of Asia, where the '**beloved disciple,' John,** had been the **Bishop,** but who had died. Who will replace him? Peter isn't available… nor any of the other disciples. But we **know** who that new Bishop was… from a letter sent from **Ignatius** in the **year 110**… to **Onesimus: Bishop of Ephesus.** An **immigrant,** trans-continental run-away slave, has become the **pastor** of the most **major church** in all of Asia. "So, might it be that some of those immigrants in your homes today could be the **future leaders of the Church in Kosovo.**" And invariably the pastors just lit up… felt renewed and so eager to continue the task of caring and loving… it was fun to see the change. I also had several rather remarkable times with some very sharp Kosovar leaders, who wanted me to come there to assist in their ministry development... tempting... ..

In the cities we visited, and in Tirana, the arenas were like those in New Orleans during Katrina... jam-packed, with just-arrived refugees... *yesterday in Vlore... last evening at dinner Ina said we have to go back to our rooms... we're not safe here after dark. Today went to the transit center—wow! Kosovars just arriving, boy and girl cousins who saw uncle killed yesterday, family raped right in front of them, all $ taken, now $0. 2000 in transit set up for 500... Ina talked with above girl, and we all stood there weeping.*

I think that God used us in a number of ways, aside from the above, as I was asked to assist in some of the administrative needs of AEP. We didn't know how long the refugee crisis would continue, but having learned the difference between relief and development, I realized that the latter could be a critical role for the future of the churches in Albania. So I began to lay out a blueprint for the churches, and AEP asked if I would stay on, **take over ACC,** and oversee long-term development. I had suggested that instead of calling it the Albania Crisis Center, we would call it the Albania Crisis & Development Center... **AC/DC** ... they of course didn't know that was a rock group in the U.S.

I was there for several months... able to email with Patti regularly... when, after U.S. intervention, the scene changed suddenly in Kosovo... the Serbs were withdrawing, and within a few weeks there was a **rapid exodus of Kosovars**... many walking... they would rather sleep on the ground in their own soil than to continue in cramped quarters. I had met with several key Albanian pastors, and they were most hopeful I would stay and assist them in carrying out their dreams… and I had to think that through… going home first for a bit, then bringing Patti back.

But sadly, the situation was little different from Bangladesh, where the foreign mission group maintained such strong control, and the nationals felt like 'less than'… I decided it would be virtually impossible to change that without a commitment to being there at least 5 years, so decided the best thing was to return.

* * * * * * * * * *

Cuba

Patti had never seen her father. Her mother had eloped in NYC with a visiting **Cuban** tobacco merchant, and he took her with him back to Cuba… she has the letter her mother sent in 1928 to **her** father, telling him all about this wonderful man. A year later, when Patti was to be born, her grandfather, **Colonel Otwell**, asked them to come to the States so she would have U.S. citizenship. The story was told that when she was born, her father saw that her eyes were **green**… not brown… and he said: **"she's not mine"…** and he went back to Cuba, leaving wife and new daughter in San Francisco. Her mother remarried… then died when Patti was 14… and in her most recent years she had been living with her grandparents.

So Patti had always lived with that gnawing question… was I not wanted? I had become aware of this, especially during our years in Chicago when I was learning to be more in touch with her 'innards.' So without telling her (in the days when calling long-distance information was free), over a period of months I made calls many evenings to every county and major city in Florida, to ask for a **Demetrio Carvajal…** response?… **0**. Then I contacted Tom Getman, former YL colleague and then Senator Mark Hatfield's right hand… and Hatfield went through the Social Security files… no Demetrio Carvajal in the U.S.

I didn't tell that to Patti, but in 2000, and a bit aware of those occasional gnawing questions, I decided that we needed to **go to Cuba** to find out. Through rather unusual circumstances, we were put in touch with a man in Miami who had grown up in **Pinar del Rio,** Patti's city of origin… about 100 miles southwest of Havana… and he put me in touch with the pastor of a church there. I knew that we had to have someone go along who was fluent in Spanish, so called Anne Barclay, a friend from our Chicago years, and who had taught in Peru for two years recently. When I called Anne, she was at Vanderbilt, taking a graduate course in Cuban Philosophical History… said **"I'd love to."**

Anne connected with us in **Cancun**, and from there we flew to **Havana**… greeted by the pastor, Rolando, who said that we would begin the next day at the **cemetery.** Arriving there, we saw **10,000 tombstones**… so where to start… when fortunately, we ran into the caretaker. "We're looking for the tombstone of Demetrio Carvajal"… "**come with me**"… and he took us right to the Carvajal Family Memorial, on which was a **picture of Demetrio, in color enamel.** That was of course a highly emotional moment for Patti… he had died in 1958 at age 50. Then we went to the Catholic church and to the place of city records, where someone said, "yes, there is a Carvajal at 84 Alameda."

So off we went, and to the door came a **very** old woman... **"yes, we know about Demetrio... come in."** The four of us entered, and before long the room was filled... another old lady... middle-aged man and woman... children... and of course all the conversation was in Spanish, so I understood nothing of what was being said. I decided we needed to find out who they were, and told Anne I wanted to do a family tree, so would be asking many questions... beginning with **"who is this elderly lady who invited us in... who is the other elderly lady...** "and on down the line. The lady 'host' was the **second wife** of Patti's granddad, and they had a son, **Pedro**... so **Patti's half-uncle,** who was there in the room... and his 3 children. The other elderly lady was Patti's granddad's **third wife**, who had a daughter, **Maria**, and she was also in the room, and her 3 children... **Patti's half-aunt.**

I wanted to get information on all of the original family, and they went down the list of the original four children... spouses and their children... with names, dates, etc., and now I had a rather complete genealogy ... holding off getting the details of Demetrio until the end. Finally about him... they said that he had married, but they had no children... "however he did have **a son** through his **servant girl, Nona"**... speaking rather derisively of her... dark-skinned 'country' girl... (they were all fair-skinned, similar to Patti.) So this would be **Patti's half-brother... Titico.**

At this point they still didn't know who we were... so then I said (all of this through Anne, of course), "and did you know that

Demetrio had been married prior to that"… **Astounding!**… so I passed around the copy of the New York City **marriage certificate** I had brought with me**. Unbelievable!!** "And, did you know that **they had a daughter**"… again looks of aghast… and I passed around Patti's **birth certificate**… father, **Demetrio**… mother, **Eunice**… **daughter, Patricia**. Again, even more jaw-dropping gasps. And then, pointing to Patti, I said: **"And this is Patricia."**

At this point Patti was a bit apprehensive, as she didn't know how they would respond, but after a few seconds Maria got up, came over to Patti, and gave her a big hug.

Rolando had already figured that we have to **find Nona,** and they indicated a general area where they thought she lived. So when we went back to his place, he got on his motorcycle… found her, and brought her to his home to meet us. In some ways Patti's life-long question of 'was I wanted?' was answered, as Nona said that when Titico was born, Demetrio had said **"now I have a son in Cuba, and a daughter in America."** She was the only person who knew about Demetrio having another child, and his statement seemed nostalgic.

Nona then called her son, who was living about 30 miles away, and said he needed to come right away… "No." "There is someone here from America to see you." "No." **"Your sister from America is here to see you."** He was there at 7 a.m. the next morning, and Patti and Titico had such a great and emotional connection… more than one person even said that they looked alike.

Patti went back two years later, and saw where Titico was living… small place, dirt floor, with his third wife and child. Patti has been back to Cuba four times… able to go with a group going on a medical mission… and we were able to get **7000 pounds** of medical supplies from an international medical agency, designated for Cuba. Titico, and later on his wife, became Christians under the influence of Rolando, and he has even been attending seminary classes. Patti and he carry on via email, to the delight of both.

A couple of years after our first trip I was invited to teach **Missions** at the Baptist seminary there in Pinar del Rio… students said it was the best class they had ever had. During that month I became very ill for a week, and fortunately, medical services in Cuba are very good.

But one of those unusual gifts from our Lord came while en-route on this trip. I had been ill prior to leaving, and was on **prednisolone**. Dumb me… I forgot it at home. Then on the flight from D.C. to Miami, I **lost it**… got woozy… vomited… passed out, and a doctor on board came and attended. Got to Miami ok, but had to get the prednisone, so we called our doctor son Steve in California to call in a prescription for 30 prednisone pills… but there was no pharmacy open at 11 p.m.… and we had a 7 a.m. flight.

When Rolando picked us up at the airport, he went to several places to get prednisone… **none.** So off to Pinar del Rio we headed… and stopped half way at this tiny spot off the road, for him to see his mother briefly. While there the prednisone thing came up… and… lo and behold… she had **30 prednisone pills** that she didn't know what to do with… not sure even why she had them... and **exactly the mg's** I needed. Patti has said at times that God protects children and fools... ...

One of the questions I raised in the Missions class was in regard to recent mission history... might it be that **God used Lenin to carry out His purposes in China?...** aware, of course, that here I was, in Cuba, a Communist country. The point was, that China had many religions... Taoism, Buddhism, Confucianism, animism, etc... and, did God use Lenin to introduce **Communism**, which could ultimately cause the influence of these other religions to dissipate?... creating a **spiritual vacuum**.

(What we know is that in **1949** there were about **1 million Christians** in China... and for the next **30** years **no Westerners** were allowed in the country. So what happened to the Church there... without any missionaries and spiritual oversight? Did it die? But we also know that 30 years later, in **1979** when the first Westerners were allowed into the country... the **lowest** estimate of the number of Christians was **40 million**... perhaps more. Did the **spiritual vacuum** created by Communism simply open minds to the new Truth? The students were intrigued with the potential local implications.)

* * * * * * * * * *

Turkey

Art Beals called again... this time to ask if Patti and I would be interested in going to **Turkey**, where the only protestant church in the city of Atalia was in need of assistance in both development and ESL. By coincidence, that pastor was going to be in California the same time we would be down there the next month, so we arranged a meeting, and it was obvious to both of us that he needed all the help he could get.

So off we went in the spring of 2002. Patti was able to be of real help in training about a dozen in teaching methods for ESL… 3 of whom were credentialed teachers of ESL… and all 3 said her input was the best they had ever experienced. For me, it was very limiting as to the development arena… they just weren't structured to carry on anything of significance. But they did ask if I would return the next year when the pastor would be gone for a year.

The following year I went back to Atalia… would be there for several months as interim for the pastor, then back again in the Spring, taking Patti with me. Although preaching would not be my primary role, I found myself enjoying that very much, and people were saying things like "wow… one of the best sermons I've ever heard"… **"you really blessed us"…** with numerous requests for a copy of a sermon. (I don't consider myself great in the pulpit… although I do have several sermons that would go well at First Church.) But I think the main thing I was able to contribute was in helping those Christians from out of the country to discover a real sense of meaning in their being there… that today's effective 'missionaries' aren't the 'professionals', but lay people such as they.

CHAPTER 19

LEARNING IS A LIFETIME

The late **Rabbi Heschel** said: "There are only three ends... **worship, love, and learning**... all else are means." I presume he meant that one doesn't do any of those three 'in order that'... i.e., they don't lead to anything else, but each is complete in itself. The latter one, **learning,** was of little interest to me in my early years... at least on the academic level, as my study habits in high school and college left much to be desired. For whatever reason, this took a turn for the better.

My first graduate course was at **Johns Hopkins University**, when we lived in Baltimore... a course in **Counseling.** Then in Wash. D.C., I took a couple of classes at Wesley Seminary... later on would take courses at Northern Baptist Seminary and Fuller Seminary (**3.8 GPA** in M.A. program!). Each study proved to be most helpful down the road, but one of the more challenging ones was at Wesley, a very liberal institution... where they told me "you don't want to come here, we're here to train men to oil the machinery." The class was for 3rd year students... **Systematic Theology.**

The prof was an incredible communicator, and his extolling of Jesus was amazing... I couldn't believe that this would come from such a liberal seminary. "Class... everything prior points to the day when Jesus Christ died for the sins of the world... everything since points back to that event... **the risen Jesus is the focal point of all history**... salvation is through him." Hey... right on! Then, about the middle of the semester, the lesson: **"7 Reasons why Christ wasn't God"**... right out of the textbook. Yikes!!! One of the basic tenets of the Christian faith has always been the deity of Christ.

Of course this is the old liberal/conservative debate, but what I had to wrestle with in my mind was... **is he a true Christian or not?** Ultimately my conclusion was twofold: 1) he had a problem with the **metaphysics** of the Trinity... as he said, e.g., in John 17... was Jesus praying to himself? But mainly... 2) here was a man so totally consumed by Jesus... and I concluded... that **we are not saved by right theology, but by faith in Jesus Christ.** It was an aha moment for me, and somewhat freeing... in not having to judge others... liberal or conservative... that it takes the whole family of God to embrace the whole Faith of God.

I felt growth in my understanding of God, and it influenced my ministry with both kids and staff... that it's not **ours** to determine who is a Christian... that Jesus himself told us to not worry about it... 'let the weeds grow up with the wheat,' and **he'd** sort it out in his good time. I began suggesting to my staff that we should never count 'numbers' as to converts at camp... that no doubt **when we get to heaven our list will differ from God's list.** It seems that evangelicals invariably use numbers for our own ego... and to raise money.

I decided I wanted to be a learner throughout my life… be stretched… discover more than I had ever imagined. My favorite epitaph, on a tombstone in London**… "Here lies Abigail Smythe, who died at the age of 103, from falling out of a cherry tree."** I saw that I learned far more when I was over my head… into new areas… and seeing life from the 'underside', where most of the world lives.

What I saw later was that the books I felt were most profitable to me weren't the 'how to' books… nor those which gave 'information'… it was those that would change/challenge my **heart**, more than my head… that God speaks more to the heart. More in the **Appendix** on readings.

CHAPTER 20

LESSONS ON LEADERSHIP

The above was the title of a series of articles in **Nation's Business** magazine. One day during my Chicago years I was thinking about leadership, and the thought came to me that I don't think I had ever thought of myself as being a leader... yet had found myself so often being put in the position of leading in various places. In high school I was put up as president of the youth ministries of the Northwest for our denomination. After just one quarter at Seattle Pacific, I was asked to run for **Student Council President**... (and when the other guy heard of that, he pulled out, but my GPA wouldn't allow me to run, so I got my close friend Ray to run... and win.) The '**Order of the S**', the letterman's club, voted me in as President, after less than one year there.

I think I was personable, energetic, and seemed to make things happen. But at one point during the Chicago years I began to sense a restless staff... and called for a 2-day Area Director conference... had us take a look at where we were going. I shared my concerns re direction, was fairly vulnerable, and they began to take me apart... basically, **not managing well.** Yes, we were going like sixty, but I was **too controlling** they said...

left some frustrated. On one occasion Neil said "you've got all those books on management in your library", and I said **"yes, but I haven't read them."** Ouch! Fortunately, they then said "we've taken Bud apart, now let's put him back together again."

That was the beginning of a journey for me, as I concluded that I had to either **not** be a Regional Director, or, learn how to manage. I began to read those books… subscribed to a different magazine every year on business… **Fortune, Forbes, Business Week**, etc. There were some things I had done well innately, but I became so aware of how much I didn't know… and decided to hone those skills. I began to see the difference between being a **leader** and a **manager.**

The process headed me toward wanting to take leadership development seriously, and I asked that every Area Director put a good figure in their annual budget for personal development, that I wanted them to become highly **capable of something beyond YL**, so they wouldn't feel trapped (as Jake had felt… 'what else can I do?') Later on one of those men told me, "every time you come to visit us, when you leave, we feel better about ourselves"… and another "you didn't give me the answers to all my questions, but **helped me figure it out.**" (Years later I realized that I had hired staff who later had become President of YL/U.S., Interim President, National Director of Training, Director of Human Resources, and the alternate for when the national Board was selecting a new President.)

Although the learning curve on management was hard and pretty steep, I think it paid off. In later years, when I passed on the baton, my successor from within the ranks wrote me a note: "You've done a top job when it comes to **guiding without**

controlling, correcting without discouraging, encouraging without flattering. It is great to be under your leadership." But the process in getting there was not easy, and very humbling at times.

The more I read and thought about leadership, the more I concluded that managerial skills can be learned… that leadership is more innate. And I concluded that people grow and develop more from connecting with people than from the classroom… Jesus **"ordained 12, *to be with him*."** Perhaps I had understood that way back… in Washington, D.C. days. During a week when **Jim Rayburn** was there, I had taken a different high school or college kid with me every day to have lunch with him, and what an incredible experience they had in meeting and being with Jim.

* * * * * * * * * *

On Mentoring

In looking back through the years, I've come to realize the significance of having a **mentor,** and what that means for one's own personal development… and I saw that God had given me some incredible mentors. Jim Rayburn had such a profound influence on Patti and me, and then in Washington, D.C. I had the privilege of being included as one of **Dick Halverson's** '12'. Later in Chicago I couldn't have had better mentors for urban ministry than **Bill Leslie** and **Ray Bakke**, both considered as two of the best in the country. And **Jim Bere'**, Chairman of Borg-Warner… considered Chicago's leading business man, became a close friend… I got him to come on YL's national Board… and I learned so much from him.

Wendell Gooch was probably the leading Trust Officer in the country... he controlled **$30 billion,** back in the '70s... taught me so much re practical matters in business... and I came to realize that mentoring is invariably **mutual.** Later, when I resigned from YL... and not knowing what I was going to do... Wendell called me from Chicago, and said "Bud, if you can do it, I can do it... the only difference is **it's going to cost me $3-4 million"...** that is what he would leave on the table from an early resignation, but said he wanted to stretch out into new and unexplored areas.

In Bangladesh I met every week for lunch with **Pastor Asish Bowl**, perhaps the second leading Bengali preacher in the country... alternating between his home and mine... what a gift for me. And in learning ministry to Muslims, **Milton Coke** met with me almost weekly for our last two years there.

In Seattle a group of 6 **black pastors** became my mentors... meeting with them every week for 6 years. **Kurt Campbell** became such a close brother... we ended up meeting almost weekly for my last 3-4 years in Seattle, and the mutuality of mentoring became so obvious... what a model for me in his heart... as owner of two auto agencies, he was probably giving up to **50% of his time** in creating innovative ministry. **Henk Wapstra** taught me so much... he had created a ministry to persons with disabilities that was as good as any in the country, a leader/teacher in ministering to today's **'lepers'**... those most of us don't like to be around... and what a gift to me not only as a personal friend, but a real mentor to me. How grateful I am for these and others, who God gave me through the years, as **models and mentors**.

* * * * * * * * * *

Perhaps the most enjoyable mentoring opportunity came with **4 college guys**... all who had come through our Young Life ministry in Hinsdale. They had been good friends in high school... all in the same grade... and the summer prior to their senior year **in college** we began to meet occasionally. I gave them the challenge of seeing that next year as a **year of growth**... including **accountability,** with each having a person on campus who would hold them accountable for spiritual disciplines.

That next summer, after graduation, the four came on 'work crew' at our YL camp in NY for the month of July, when I was camp director. Then they agreed to being with each other **for the next year**... have a job, and also be involved in some sort of ministry. I arranged for each of them to have a **business man** as a **mentor**... meet with that person at least once a month. And the five of us met **every Sunday night**, for the entire year... Bible study, and lots of fun in just being together.

The next thing I did was to ask a number of people who they thought were the 5 or 6 **most influential** Christians in the Chicago area... called the 7 who were mentioned the most, and asked if they would give an evening to these men... share their **faith journey**... **successes**... **struggles**... and all 7 agreed, most of them inviting us into their home for dinner and an evening. What a great treat it was for these 4 guys to hear the intimate hearts of 7 community leaders, and stalwarts of the faith.

Then I arranged for us to go to the annual **Prayer Breakfast** in Wash., D.C... and also to meet with a number of Christian leaders there, including a session with **John Stott** on the way. On Friday night **Jim Wallis** hosted us in his (spartan) home for dinner... and then **Dick Halverson** hosted us for lunch on Saturday at the Kenwood Country Club... what a contrast.

Only God knows the effect all that had on those men, but today, each has a strong faith being lived out in their career... one a successful attorney in North Carolina... another heads up a counseling center for indigents in Denver... a third resigned last year from the Gates Foundation as Director of Education Evaluation... and the fourth had recently resigned as Deputy Secretary of Treasury in Wash., D.C.

CHAPTER 21

BAPTISTS

In 2003 our granddaughter, Nashira, was married, and she and Jim moved to Portland, where he had grown up... and Nashira said to Patti and me "would you guys come live near us?" So we did... but there's a **story behind the story** (as Paul Harvey would say) of moving to Portland at Nashira's request... as we had developed a rather unusual relationship.

In 1999, a month or two prior to my going to Albania... out of the blue came an email from Nashira, who was then living in Hawaii. **"Grampa... what was the message of Jesus?"** This from one who had been to church maybe once in her 23 years... wow!... where's this coming from? We wrote back and forth a couple of times, but then I'm off to Albania. A couple months later she called Patti, to ask about what happens when a person becomes a Christian... and do they change names? Someone she knew, a Catholic, was going to be baptized, and would take a new name... so??? Patti spoke briefly of that, but then said to her "I should let grampa tell you this, **but he baptized you when you were a baby."** "He did?... no wonder I've been spared so many bad things." Remarkable!

So when I returned from Albania, the first thing I suggested to Patti was that we go to Hawaii, to see Nashira… and I would share the story, which of course she never knew.

In 1976 Cherie was living with John, south of Tucson, and she had called to announce the arrival of her daughter. I was on my sabbatical, and heading to California, so I would stop and see them… our first grandchild. They picked me up at the airport, and we headed south… then east up into the hills… then off into little lanes through dry gulches… out to the middle of nowhere, where two or three couples were living. Cherie kept talking about 'good energy'… and as I would walk around with this new child in my arms, praying for her, I said "Cher, I'm giving her '**good energy**'… and she would say "**way to go, dad.**" It was a good time with them, but a couple of days later when it came time for me to leave, I realized I hadn't done what Patti had suggested… "be sure to '**dedicate' the baby.** So half an hour before I was to leave, I felt I needed to do that… but where?

I went out the back door, and there on a cement platform was a washing machine, with **water** on the cement… and the thought hit me so clearly and strongly… **I'm going to baptize her.** But where? So I walked across toward a barn, where a goat was standing in the doorway… went over there, and in the back corner of the goat pen was one of those big old tubs, half full of water. It was just so clear… **'that's it'**… and I slid across the goat pen to that tub, holding this 3-week old in my arms.

Now for Presbyterians, baptisms are usually done by 'sprinkling', and I knew that one **never** baptizes someone alone… it is always done with the family, and in front of the **congregation.** But there was never a single thought of this not being right… and as I looked back on it later, felt so strongly that **these were not my thoughts or words**, but from God. I reached down, took some water, sprinkled it on her head, and said "Nashira Dawn, in the name of the Father, and of the Son, and of the Holy Spirit, I baptize you… and **may the day come when you will come to know Jesus as Lord… and may you be an influence in the life of your mother."**

But the amazing thing was that **I was not alone**… I can still hear it… **singing… chorus** from a **huge host** of God's people **right there in the goat pen with us…** I felt surrounded! I know those weren't my thoughts or doings… those actions, and words, were **from God**. I was not in control… He was… and I was simply **living HIStory.**

So when we went to Kauai to see them, I shared that story with Nashira… and then told her that I was going to share it also with her mother, which I did. It was a great few days… Nashira stayed with us overnight a couple of times… and Patti and I headed back.

A month or so later I got an email from Nashira… **"Grampa, last night I prayed to the Father… confessed all my sins… told Him I wanted to follow Jesus, have a life that is clean and pure… and it felt good."** She moved to Honolulu to do some college work, and then about five years ago, Cherie went there to see her. Nashira had earlier gone on a mission trip to Fiji with IV… was now going to join a church… and there would be a meeting on Friday night and much of Saturday, discussing what baptism and joining the church meant. Cherie went with Nashira that Friday evening, and while they were singing, made comment that **'these are the songs I grew up with'**... same on Saturday... said to Nashira **"that's what I want"**... and we have the video of **the 2 of them being baptized together.** ("and may you be an influence in the life of her mother"... God's words)

Later, Nashira would come to Seattle and graduate from Seattle Pacific University. She had asked us about what should be her major, and I told her "Art, of course"... she is an extremely gifted artis**t. "But how can I use that for God?"...** to which I responded: **"**Do you know the first time **gifts of the Spirit** are mentioned in the Bible?... in **Exodus 31**, where "the Holy Spirit gave the **gift of art** and craftsmanship for the building of the tabernacle to... "and names 2 men. They would be building a tabernacle in the **middle of the desert**... and, as Martin Luther said, "the poor need beauty as much as bread, because they live among ugliness." She majored in art, and the prof said that she set the bar so high for others in the class... her senior project was a major focus of all the displays.

A couple of years later Nashira got married... Jim had grown up in Portland, with strong roots and ties there, and that's where they would move to. So prior to their moving, she asked if we would move there, and since I could do in Portland what I was doing in Seattle... we moved.

CHAPTER 22

BACK TO PORTLAND

I decided to pursue in Portland what I had initiated in Seattle… finding ways to address human needs … and how can the Church be engaged in this. I asked several people 'who was doing what in the city,' and was told to get in touch with **Mariah Taylor**… an African-American nurse. What an amazing clinic she was running… the North Portland Nurse Practitioner Community Health Clinic, the only clinic in the city providing health services for **children of un-insured families**… treated several thousand each year… over **1000** of them **free** the year before. In meeting her one is impressed with commitment and charisma … honored by **Oprah** in 2000, and recently by the Portland mayor, for 25 years of outstanding service.

When I met her, we clicked well, and in learning she had only one person on her Board, I told her I'd help develop that, which I did… ended up with a strong group of twelve… **half minority**… some prominent people. Several months later the front office staff gal resigned, and, sensing a problem, I asked her to write me a letter as to why… learned that her predecessor had also resigned, and asked her to write also. In both cases… **terrible abuse**… insults, yelling, etc. In one instance one of them had an arm punctured from a used needle Mariah threw toward the sink... then blamed her for getting in the way. I showed these letters to the attorney on our Board, and he said that in our knowing of the abuses, we could be **sued if we did nothing**. Later we learned that the Health Dept. hadn't wanted to inspect the Clinic... they'd have to shut it down, with adverse effects on too many children.

About the same time I heard that former Board persons had also had the same abuse from Mariah, and I asked them to write... 5 did, and the abuses were extreme and absurd... as well as Mariah unwilling to do anything the Board asked, and spending indiscriminately. No wonder strong Boards in the past had been reduced to only one member. We realized we had a tiger by the tail, and I learned that all the other staff experienced the same abuse... but stayed out of concern for children.

What followed was a judicious effort by the Board to first ask her to relinquish her role as Executive Director... where she was extremely deficient... but she strongly resisted. We pursued mediation... offered a substantial retirement package... and when she resisted all we engaged a human resources agency to provide an objective evaluation. Their conclusion?... she <u>cannot</u> return to the Clinic... but she rejected that. Inquiries were made by the press, but we simply said **"no comment"**... actually wanting to protect Mariah ... did not want to be vindictive. I was vilified in all the papers for "**firing the Mother Theresa of Portland**"... received letters and phone calls. But for me the most sad aspect was that this 'Christian' woman, so highly recognized in her church... was hated by staff.

After 8 months of very laborious efforts toward some sort of mutual benefit, we officially terminated her... changed the name to the **Children's Community Clinic**... moved it to a much better facility nearby... hired a person to take over, and it's going great. Then I began to receive calls and notes from a variety of people... **"thanks"**... **"finally."**

* * * * * * * * * *

During our first year in Portland I was invited to be the speaker at Warner Pacific College's Faculty Lecture Series... chose to use the student theme of the year **"Beyond the World of Me."** The first chapel talk I titled **"Leprosy in Portland"**, and spoke of our leprosy work in Bangladesh... and the historic concept of **"unclean."** And who might those people be here in Portland... the ones we all want to **avoid?** In Seattle I had been closely involved with two different ministries to persons with disabilities, and they would say that **persons with disabilities** are the **most avoided people** in society... no one likes to be around them... we don't know how to interact with them. I had learned from a city agency there are about **150,000** with disabilities in metro Portland... and, they are also the most unchurched group there is. So, does today's Church care about the most needy in society?

I was invited to a faculty luncheon... asked the question "how can **Warner** make a difference in the city?" After some discussion on this, I asked how they would describe the area immediately south of the campus ... **"low-income, multi-ethnic."** So my response to their question was to not think of the **city,** but to **"think small** in a **big way**... what difference can Warner make in the next 10 years in a 40-square block area right next to your campus?" The Sociology students could do their term papers on the demographics, etc... all of that information is readily available... but mainly, it could put students in direct contact with people living in the area... **people, not programs**, influence others.

They asked me to assist them in addressing the above... gave me an office... and I began meeting with Principals, community leaders, etc... and initiated an ESL program in one of the elementary schools... who asked Warner the following year to help **train their teachers** in Spanish.

* * * * * * * * * *

There were several different groups with which I connected... ministry to **homeless street kids** (Portland has the highest percent of street kids in the country)... a group of key **business leaders,** whose goal is "the spiritual transformation of leaders, and the cultural transformation of the city"... and several others. I contacted several large churches, with the idea of **"adopt a classroom"...** to see what collective impact can be made by a number of churches taking that on in their community. One outreach director of a large church told me "we'd love to, but would probably not do that with other churches." That was the attitude I saw more than once in this city, and **Murdock Trust** said that was also their experience... that groups don't seem to work with each other here. This was most discouraging to me, as our experience in Seattle was one of such great mutual participation in ministering to a city. In several conversations with leaders, they told me of city-wide efforts here that had come... **and gone.**

* * * * * * * * * *

Lifestyle

One of the difficult things in moving to a new city is to find that church where one feels most nourished… but it is even more difficult to 'fit in' as one grows older. We attended a Presbyterian church for a year… the pastor had me preach a couple of times so the people would get to know us. But so much was ingrown, and it just didn't seem to have much oomph.

One Sunday I heard a preacher who was sooo good… Baptist church… but could we ever become **Baptists?** We began to attend, and last summer, 2007, we joined a small group from that church. They were having discussions from a book they were reading on stewardship, and that first evening we attended it was on **life-style.** When Patti and I returned home that evening, we talked about that… and the oft-used term of **'simple** life-style.' It seemed to us that was such a **relative term**… depending on where one is coming from. My comment to Patti was that it seemed to me the more appropriate question would be… what was a **biblical life-style**… what would that look like, even in today's world?

We talked about that at length, and concluded that, at the least, God would have life lived at a **comfort level**… didn't think He would say one should intentionally live at a level of discomfort… certainly Bangladesh was not exactly comfortable… which again, is so relative. In moving from Seattle, we had wanted a **home with a view** (in Seattle we had an unobstructed view of Puget Sound and the Olympic mountains). So I hit the computer… **Portland West Hills**… **View** and purchased a lovely home at the top of the hill... and got a gorgeous view... **plus a 3-level garden.**

As we discussed 'life-style', we concurred that we were definitely living **above a comfort level,** and after a bit Patti asked if I was willing to give up the view... **"yes."** So then my question to her... was she willing to give up the beautiful, vaulted-ceiling master bedroom and bath we had done in extensive renovations... **"yes."** We mutually decided right then and there that we could comfortably live with less... would move ... buy **'down'**, and have more funds to assist those less-fortunate... felt good. We put our home up for sale... looked at maybe 15-20 homes, and then saw one where we both said **'this is it,'** and bought it. We were aware that the housing market had become rather shaky, but felt this was the right thing to do, even before selling our present home... later rented it.

8/6/07 Long time since I've journaled —haven't felt the need to, and probably just lazy. But recent occasions in Scripture have piqued my heart/mind... sort of challenging me to get with it more. Several things I've realized this past year — Portland is a different place, and people do their own thing more. Even Murdock says that. And, I don't have a Jonathan, someone to walk alongside, with kindred heart... not fun to be alone in what I'm doing.

Also, I realize that I'm much more motivated spiritually when I'm part of a team, doing that which is challenging, and needing God's strength and wisdom to carry it out. I think I've become sort of casual/fatalistic—just figuring that at my age there's nothing to prove, so what the heck. Will just deal with matters as they arise. The Clinic has been the main thing, and that may end up for me this week. Mixed feelings... getting more comfortable with actually retiring... and yet feeling there's much more I can give. But where?

Patti and I want to be biblical in how we live---may be easier to do that materially than spiritually---what are the implications of the latter? Should we go overseas for a stretch? This house thing brings some uncertainty— do we sell?... rent???

So last night as I read in Ezekiel... "I will reaffirm my covenant with you... despite all you have done, I will be kind to you again... forgive you all that you have done." Now a new start on tomorrow??? Lord, help me... and be "completely at home with you" as was said of Moses in his walk with God.

* * * * * * * * * *

In our discussion about passing on what could be a substantial sum, Patti had said her interest was in **young girls** and **needy mothers** in **Africa**... so we decided we'd look into who was doing something effective there, but who had **limited access to U.S. funding**. That began a search, and after **scores** of phone-calls and emails... and from a phone conversation with a friend in Philadelphia ... who referred me to someone in Pasadena... who was in Nairobi when I emailed her... we learned of **Life In Abundance.** It was founded by a **Kenyan** woman doctor, headquartered in **Ethiopia**, and they are now in **5** African countries... operating on a very small budget. I had also been in touch with Gary Edmonds, the former Director of the World Evangelical Alliance, who put us in touch with his key man in **Rwanda.**

Last Fall I read the book *The Bottom Billion*... showing that **one-sixth** of the population of the world will never make it...

and **70%** of those are in **Africa**. In my mind I find that my world of 'yesterday' was one of thinking of the Third World as 'out there'… it's **their** problems, not mine. But we now know that *The World is Flat,* as Friedman says, and so much today has global implications, even for me/us. So I am challenged by what that means for us… who is my neighbor? And In Ephesians Paul says "of whom the **whole family** is named… "So, if **I** am actually **related** to t**hem…** ("God, please leave me alone… I've been doing just fine.")

By an **accident of birth**, I'm an American… so blessed in every way. But I also realize that God blessed Israel **"to be a blessing"**, as he told Abraham… and they didn't, so his blessing left them. And with America having **5%** of the world's population, but consuming **40%** of the world's goods… it's obvious to most that we've lavished those blessings more on ourselves than on others. And "to whom much is given, will much be required." But I've also discovered what I learned in athletics… that **it's so much more fun to play than to watch**… even if I lose… and participating in God's agenda is so much more fulfilling than… uh… playing golf… which I've always loved. (For **23 years** my 3 boys and I never missed a summer without a game of golf together… took a week off one year in San Jose and played **8** rounds of 18-hole golf those 5 days.)

So last February Patti and I went to **Ethiopia,** and were so impressed by what Life In Abundance is doing, with so little… the only ministry that I've ever seen whose aim is primarily to **empower the local church** for outreach and community change. They are committed to helping them with funds and training for three years, and then have them on their own… started nine years ago, and now are involved with **20 churches** in Addis

Ababa, plus many in other cities of Ethiopia, plus the other countries. We saw one church that had just begun... a school of **25** children, but with **0** playground or other equipment... then visited a school going for 6 years... beautiful!... we saw what could be. (I visited the Director of one of the large Christian agencies in Addis, whose budget this year is $46 million.)

We flew to **Rwanda** for a week-end... wow!... what they have gone through. We visited the Memorial (I felt like John the Baptist... preceding George Bush by 2 days), which shows the gruesome details of the incredible ethnic cleansing of **Tutsis by the Hutus**... who murdered almost one million in just a few months. And then we met with members of both groups... and witnessed some of the amazing reconciliation that is going on.

We attended the service of a **church for prostitutes**... more than **100** of them. Since the majority of the Tutsi women had their husbands murdered, how do they feed themselves and their children? But a score or more have become Christians... even though some still ply their trade. I asked our host about other means of providing income, and he mentioned several options, one of which would be a mill for grinding grain, to sell. I communicated with Gary Edmonds, and he sent the schemata for what that would provide... less than **$1500** would create a **living wage** for **94 women** within **3 years**... it's already begun.

One of our interests in going to Africa was to see if there might be something in which we could participate... perhaps go for 1-3 months once or twice a year. We found that Patti could be kept busy 24/7 teaching ESL... but I didn't see anything with my name on it. A seminary in Addis invited us to come, but it would have been for a longer term than we wanted.

CHAPTER 23

BACK ... AND FORTH

So now in our 'sunset' years, we look back with great appreciation for how God has blessed in so many ways. How much we've enjoyed our 4 children through the years... each was in their dad's YL club, with their many friends. Cherie, Pete and Phil were all on a work crew at one of the YL camps... Cherie in Colorado, and Pete and Phil in NY. It was fun (well, for the most part) in watching them grow up... finish high school, then meandering through various stages of college... and then being involved in a variety of interesting careers and life-changes.

Even though they've lived quite distant from us after college years... **Cherie** in Tucson and Hawaii... **Pete** in Seattle and Frankfurt... **Phil** in New Orleans... and **Steve** in California... we've been able to spend time with them in each place. And, we've all been together many different years. Now Cherie has moved to Portland, and Phil is spending more time in the Seattle area... (he came to visit us for a weekend a couple of years ago... arrived on Friday... **Katrina** hit on Sunday... he stayed 2 months.)

Cherie's other daughter, **Alora,** had moved from Hawaii to Southern California... then moved here to Portland... so we've enjoyed so much seeing her more. Pete and Linda adopted 3 children... **Aaron** as a baby when they were in Frankfurt... and later back in Seattle, 2 whose parents were dying from AIDS, both of them now out of school... **Erica** in San Diego, and **Kevin** just out of the Marines after a stint in Iraq... I flew to North Carolina in January to drive him home. When Pete and his 3 were living in Olympia we saw them often. And we usually went to California a couple of times a year to see Steve and his 2... **Sophia** and **Sasha.** One disappointment for both of us is that we've always lived so far away from our grandkids... would have loved to be with them more often.

Our health is generally good... with the normal aches and pains of the years. Two weeks before we moved to Portland, I developed **atrial fibrillation**... heart rate went from my normal 52 to 88, and irregular. Through a close friend I was accepted as a patient by a good internist, and after some months of getting the thyroid regulated, a cardiologist recommended **cardio-version**... then heart back to 55, and regular. In light of my family history, the doc has some concerns... my **dad** died of a sudden heart attack at age 63... **Perk** died at the wheel at age 45... and my twin, **Pat**, died also at the wheel, at age 63. (So I let Patti drive.) But my Seattle doc said I have my mother's genes... she and all of her siblings lived into their 90's. But having faced 'the future' twice... it's all in God's hands. I like the paraphrase of Paul... "for to me to live, is to have Christ... to die, is to have more of Christ."

So now what's ahead for me... for Patti? I've said for a number of years that it feels so good to not have to '**count**'... don't have to 'succeed' in anything I do... it's so freeing... could play golf every day (if my knee would let me), and not feel guilty. And yet both of us feel that there may be those places where our experience could be of help... life is so much more fun in finding ways to come along side of those who have so much less than we.

In the Gospel of John, Jesus several times speaks of "I only do what the Father tells me"... which means he's a **responder,** more than an initiator. Almost all my life I've been an **initiator**... have been blessed beyond what I would have ever dreamed. So now it's good to be a responder... awaiting whatever it is that God has for me... for us. I continue receiving calls asking for assistance from a variety of sources here in the city... currently invited by a couple of the city's larger churches to help them develop non-profits as a means for increased outreach... but content to '**just be.**' In the past 10-15 years I've served on more than 15 Boards... some nationally... and have enjoyed being part of the process of perhaps contributing in some small ways to a variety of Kingdom efforts.

If there's one thing that remains heavy on my heart... it's the inability of the evangelical church in America to give itself strongly to the '**have-nots**'... to only superficially care about those with whom Jesus would be if he were here today. In Seattle there was one church, Plymouth Congregational... considered a very liberal church... that was doing more for housing for the poor than all the evangelical churches collectively in metro Seattle. It seems that **Matthew 25** is primarily theory. I remind myself on occasion of that intriguing brief comment by **David** in Ps. 18... "He stooped down to make me great." And it seems to me the task of the Church is to stoop down, to uplift the lowly.

We could be nostalgic re the past… apprehensive about the future… but both are beyond our power to control… and so we can relax, knowing it is all in Christ's hands.

Patti and I feel blessed in so many ways… God has enriched our lives so wonderfully… with each other, and with such a legion of friends along the way… you reading this are probably one of those… who have loved us… cared and encouraged in so many ways… so I simply say… **THANKS!!!**

PATTI

This treatise can't be complete without comment about the greatest gift God ever gave me... my wonderful wife. As I expressed earlier, for so many years I wasn't skilled or mature enough to know how to connect with her in meaningful ways, and yet she was so incredibly loving and supportive to me. And she was so good in providing a 'home' for the kids... always there, with **lots of love.**

I know so very well that without Patti's deep involvement in many of the things I did, they would **never** have gone so well. In YL she almost always **mentored** a group of gals... especially in Chicago... and her ability to organize a group of women and put on a **banquet for 500**... amazing.

What emerged was a woman who began to discover her own gifts... of listening... of teaching... of loving... of creating... and eventually what I saw was that when she had a **vision** for something, **I knew it would happen**. As the TV commercial says: "**I guarantee it.**" One of those early ones was the tutoring program in Chicago's Cabrini... where out of nothing, she recruited 25 tutors... trained them... would be alone at night where no white person would ever be, and was never afraid. That program grew to where later it had a $1million budget.

In Bangladesh, after a couple of years of angst in not finding a niche, she created what became considered the best English learning center in the country… **trained 4 Bengalis**, brought in another expat… and had 50 people on a waiting list. Her male Bengali teacher once said to her… **"you have changed me completely … I've been overwhelmed by love."** Two years after we left they had her come back to help start a second school.

In Seattle she decided that she wanted to get into **ESL**, so took a 4-week graduate course from Seattle U. for accreditation. Then she went to **China 5 summers,** mostly teaching university professors **English-teaching methods**… also to **Kyrgyzstan** and **Turkey**, where several who already had their ESL certification said it was the best stuff they had ever learned. At the request of World Relief, she taught newly arrived immigrants, who could speak **0 English…** with some getting jobs after just **2 weeks. S**he was **good.** She set up tutor-training programs for the **entire city**… oversaw all the tutoring programs for Catholic Community Services… wrote a tutor-training manual, published by Washington Mutual…

When we were at Bethany, Patti spent a year or more in being tutored in the ministry of **healing prayer…** then initiated that at our church, which continues with strong influence. She and Gracie Mitchell set up a much needed and effective program for bringing **newcomers** into the church. At the 4,000 member **University Presbyterian Church** she taught the class on healing prayer… also classes on the **Spiritual Classics.** As I said above… I learned that whenever Patti took on a task, I knew it would happen with great effect.

Her **long-suffering patience** with me... which continues... has been remarkable. But I especially respect and admire her in her **love for Jesus.** She has been such a model to me... in her devotional life... in her desire to be fully Jesus' person. I can only say that my life has been embellished so wonderfully by her love... her care... by her example... and **I have been most blessed**. We have learned to love each other so deeply... and to laugh together... and life for me would be so much less without her... **Thank you, my dear!!!**

Appendixes

DIVINE INTERVENTIONS

A number of events occurred during my life that showed me that God's serendipity care guides, heals, and provides for His followers. Here is a summary of a few noteworthy examples from my life that I previous mentioned.

1. In 1954 our family of four was living in Philadelphia in a duplex with our belongings. We were preparing to move to Baltimore, but first we had to visit Seattle with two months left on our lease. We didn't have the money to pay for the two months, so I put an ad in the newspaper to sublease the unit. Two weeks went by and nobody had called about it. But I was not worried, and the morning we were to leave, I got a call. A man said he had seen the ad when it first appeared and wanted to know if it was still available. I said yes, and he came over to the house. He agreed to take it, living with our furnishing in it. He gave us money for two months of rent, I paid the landlord, and we left on our 2-month trip.

2. Young Life did not pay well. Staff were responsible for raising their own support, and while we were living in Baltimore, I had little income. On Christmas eve in 1957, we had no food in the house, so there would be nothing to

eat Christmas morning, but I didn't tell anybody about it. In the morning when I went to get the newspaper on the front porch, a big bag of groceries was sitting there next to the paper.

3. Our family moved to California in 1960, and eventually I became a Young Life Area Director in San Jose. In 1965 I was missing the east coast culture but wondered if I should stay in California. I wanted God's guidance on the matter, so I knelt to pray about it in the living room. I asked God, "Should I stay or should I go? How will I know?"

    I heard a clear voice: "Scripture." I responded, "Where?" The voice in my mind spoke again: "Mark 10." I continued praying and kept hearing "**Mark 10**." I grabbed the Bible that sat on the coffee table and looked up Mark 10. I didn't get past the first phrase, which began, "And after he left that place …" I said to God, "thank you!"

    But I didn't know where to go. I was considering a move to Detroit or Buffalo and took a trip to Detroit. It didn't feel right, and Bob Mitchell asked me to consider becoming the Regional Director in southern California. I told him I didn't want to be a Regional Director and I didn't want to live in southern Cal. Bob told me, "Go take a look."

    So I flew south and met the Young Life staff in the region. They were all in therapy and asked me, "Are you going to change us?" I told them that it's not my job to change anybody—that's God's job. I couldn't wait to get out of there and return home. But as my plane took off over the city of Los Angeles, I looked down at the sprawl and had an overwhelming feeling that "these are my people" and this was to be my home. So we moved.

4. After four years as the Regional Director for southern California, Bill Star, the YL President, asked to move to the Great Lakes Region to oversee Young Life operations in Illinois, Indiana, Michigan, and Wisconsin. He needed a good manager of people in the position, so in the summer of 1969, we moved to Hinsdale in the western suburbs of Chicago. It was known for its excellent schools and was the home of many senior executives who worked in Chicago. Different areas of the region subsidized my salary, but I still needed to raise funds for my own living expenses. I usually did this by requesting financial support from a few of my wealthy friends. But in 1977, I decided not to tell anybody about my financial needs and see what would happen. I needed to raise at least $10,000 to meet my support needs.

Lisa Tieszen, one of the kids in my Hinsdale club, told me her parents wanted to give money to Young Life and wanted to know how to do it. I told her it depended on how much he would give. In some cases, it was done locally, but for large sums, donations should be sent to the YL headquarters. I left it at that. A short time later, a check arrived at headquarters for $96,000 from the Tieszens. Of this amount, $10,000 was designated to support the YL camps and another $10,00 was to support Tom Moucka, a local guy who was going on staff from the Hinsdale area. The rest ($76,000) was designated for my support. The extra amount would come in handy when I moved to Portland in less than a year, and it covered my expenses until I established contacts in Oregon.

Shortly after receiving the Tieszen gift, Jane Landis, the mother of Emily who was another kid in the Hinsdale club, came down with spinal meningitis, a deadly infection of the brain and spinal cord, and encephalitis, an inflammation of the brain. (Those with mild symptoms may recover in 2-4 weeks, but those with severe symptoms may die or be permanently impaired.) The two families were close friends, and I had previously had both illnesses that caused me to take a year off of work and move from Maryland to California. I went to see Jane in the hospital and told her I previous had both illnesses, but God was gracious and I was totally healed. I held her hand and prayed with her.

That evening, I asked God to take the generosity of the Tieszen family and transfer it into healing for Jane. I clearly heard a YES and then felt a shock go through my body. I said, "Thank you." Jane was back at work in two weeks, fully functioning and feeling perfectly fine.

5. In the summer of 1977, I was driving a bus full of Hinsdale YL kids back from Malibu, a camp in British Colombia. On a narrow road near Fargo, ND, a large truck approached us. I moved onto the shoulder of the road to let him by. But the shoulder was soft and the weight of the bus caused it to cave in and slowly suck the bus off the road. Eventually, the bus started going down the bank and eventually came to rest just past a cement drainage ditch (2 feet wide, 1 foot deep) part way down the hill. I felt no bump as the bus came to a stop. When the tow truck driver arrived, he asked me, "How did the bus get over here?" The bus wheel was on the other side of the ditch and the bus should have turned over and tumbled down the hill when we hit the ditch, but there

were no bus tracks from one side of the ditch to the other where the bus had stopped. I told him, "We will never know how this happened." I became convinced there are guardian angels watching out for us.

6. When we decided to move to Portland in 1977 so we could be closer to Patti's family, I had to buy a house. I flew there for a few days and looked at many houses, knowing I needed to buy one during the trip. I heard about one in the SW hills with a nice view of the valley, and I really liked it. However, it was still in the process of being put on the market. I talked to the agent and asked how much the seller wanted for the house, but was told the price wasn't established yet. I made an offer and a local doctor also made the same offer. He offered all cash, but I would need to get a loan and wasn't approved for a loan yet. The agent asked if I could meet an earlier closing date, and I said yes. She said, "It's yours." She accepted by personal check from an Illinois bank as earnest money and the deal was done, beating the all-cash offer from the local doctor.

7. I was driving from Bend, Oregon to Eugene for a Young Life staff meeting on November 16, 1978. It was very cold but clear, and I was driving 70 mph on a straight-away of the highway and was passing a truck. I didn't know about "black ice" and I eventually found myself passing the truck going sideways. I hit a dry patch which spun me around and took me off the road. The car hit a big tree sideways at the post right behind the driver's door, folding the car in two, and it came to rest in the bushes. I had an out-of-body experience as I felt myself twirling upward in a spiral and thinking, "I'm going to beat you home, Patti."

Then I don't remember anything. If the car had hit the tree at my door (one foot away), I would have been killed instantly. I wasn't wearing my seat belt, and after the truck driver called for an ambulance, I was found on the ground in the bushes with one leg still in the car. I had broken 15 bones, mostly in my back, but also my hip and several ribs. The ambulance trip to Bend, followed by the med-evac helicopter ride to Portland, were very painful. I was in the hospital for 10 days while they put me into traction for the long healing process. Howard Blessing rigged up a rope to a beam in the open ceiling so I could lift myself up and sit in bed. After being discharged, I was in pain every time I took a step.

We were attending West Hills Covenant Church in SW Portland and Randy Roth was the senior pastor. During communion six months after the accident, he invited members of the congregation to come forward if they wanted prayer while the other pastor administered communion. I decided to go forward. Randy asked me, "What do you want prayer for?" I said, "I can't take a step or bend over without pain." Randy put some oil on my wrist and prayed quietly while the congregation sang songs. I don't remember what he said, and when he said Amen, I limped slowly back to my seat.

When I was home later that day, I dropped something and bent over to get it. When I stood back up, I realized I had bent over without any pain. I said to myself, "I just bent over and it didn't hurt." I bent over several more times to see if I would be in pain, and the pain was gone. Then I just started laughing. The pain never returned.

8. Patti and I went to Cuba in 2002 after we found her relatives in Pinar del Rio a few years earlier. I had been ill and realized on the flight to DC that I had forgotten my Prednisolone (a prescription of 30 pills of 5 mg each). I got very sick on the flight from DC to Miami, and I figured we would get a replacement prescription in Miami by having my son Steve (a doctor) write one for me. But after we arrived late that evening, we couldn't find a pharmacy that was open. I figured we would get it in Havana. We flew to Havana early the next morning, and we were met by our driver who would take us to Pinar del Rio, about 100 miles west of Havana where Patti's father had lived. We told him we first needed to find a pharmacy so I could get my medication. But the driver was not from Havana and he couldn't find a pharmacy that had it.

    While we traveled, the driver stopped at his house in a little village 30 miles east of Pinar del Rio. He apologized to his mother for being late—we had taken time to look for a pharmacy and he still had not delivered us to our destination. His mother asked him what we needed, and he told her I needed Prednisolone. She said, "I have some. I don't know where it came from or when I got it." She got the bottle from her medicine cabinet and gave it to him to give to me. It was a bottle of 30 pills with 5 mg each, my exact prescription.

MISCELLANEOUS MUSINGS

In the process of writing these memoirs, I was encouraged to include miscellaneous thoughts and a list of some books that have meant a lot to me. Through the years I've read at times about a book a week… found it enjoyable to read 2 or 3 at the same time. But in the last 15-20 years, I've noticed that those which were most meaningful to me were the ones that gave **insight** more than information… spoke more to the **heart** than the head. Each of these listed has had a strong influence on my life at one point or another… so, not in any particular order.

- **John Gardner** – *Self Renewal*, one of the early books I read on risking and not worrying about failing
- **Elizabeth O'Connor** – all her books are about the life of Church of the Savior, Wash., D.C.
- **Batten & Hudson** – *Dare to Live Passionately*… a great encouragement to me to live on the edge
- **Kenneth Bailey** – *The Cross & the Prodigal*… the best exegesis there is on Luke 15
- **Jan Vanier** – *Be Not Afraid*… not a book for the comfort zone
- **Henri Nouwen** – all his books… especially enjoyed *Gracias* … read it while in Bangladesh
- **Juan Carlos Ortiz** – *Disciple*… I've given it to several who in turn have given out hundreds

- **Blaise Pascal** – *Pensees...* an amazing compendium of practical living and thinking
- **McNeill, Morrison, Nouwen** – *Compassion...* like Vanier, challenging
- **Dale Bruner** – *Commentary on Matthew* (2 vols.)... best there is, used it for daily devotions.

I have kept just 100 books... felt that if I wasn't going to read a book again, it could be of more use to someone else. So I've given away maybe 2000 books... to individuals, college libraries, etc. (Basically, I'm lazy... don't want to keep packing books in boxes for when I move, then never open them... it's happened more than once.)

* * * * * * * * * *

This section consists of some random thoughts... some perhaps having been an influence on how I think... feel... make decisions. Then there are notes I made for myself along the way, on **Risking & Renewal**... looking at them on occasion to maintain perspective.

From the life of David... who knew he was to become king, and king Saul was trying to kill him. When David and his friends were hiding deep in a cave, and Saul fell asleep in the entrance, David's friends told him to kill Saul... "see, God has delivered him to you."
- favorable circumstances are not necessarily providential
- the counsel of friends may not always be correct.

Jan Vanier speaks of those whose *"minds are more developed than their hearts."*

"The Church exists by mission as a fire exists by burning." *Wm. Temple*

God says: "I change not"… He will always be **unpredictable**… and that won't change

"Without community, **faith limps**, it doesn't run." *Roberta Hestenes*

What is **cultural** and what is **biblical** in my lifestyle?

"You need a person with whom you feel free to be insecure." *Henri Nouwen*

God chooses at times to allow negative experiences to bring about His good for us.

From a national leader such as Jim Bere, confirmed in *Blink*… **go with your gut**… your heart.

"The leader's first task is always to define reality… see with clarity." *Max De Pree*

"Prayer is not a pious decoration of life but the breath of human existence." *Nouwen*

"Never let your reading get ahead of your experience." (Forget who)

"I love poverty, because He loved it. I love riches, because they afford me the means of helping the very poor." *Pascal*

"Jesus Christ and St. Paul employ the rule of love, not of intellect; for they would warm, not instruct."` *Pascal*

"It is the Cross which determines how I look at people... not ethnicity." *John Howard Yoder*

God says: "I change not" ... He will remain being **unpredictable** ... and that won't change.

* * * * * * * * * *

RISKING AND RENEWAL

The history of Christianity is a history of people who took risks... growth occurs not in the comfort zone, but in obedience to God's call to join in 'out there'

Faith without risk is no faith at all... **faith doesn't rescue** us, **but guides** us (Heb. 11)

We risk for 2 reasons: 1) for the sake of others, and 2) for our own sake... there is no growth without risk

Newness comes from within – the Spirit of God is a creative person, who invites us to **dream, create, imagine, innovate,** bringing freshness, new insights, greater degrees of caring in every area of life

The greatest element in risk has to do with my heart being close enough in touch with God's heart that I'm able to hear His "no" – and I'm betting everything I know and have on the security of His love for and commitment to me

Risk is like a trapeze – it's when I let go of what I'm holding on to... but with the assurance of that which will hold me when I let go

Risking may involve more what one leaves behind than what one goes to – planned neglect may be the secret of success

Jesus promised His followers at least 3 things:
- they'd be **absurdly happy** (John 10:10)
  - they'd be **completely fearless** (the "fear not"s)
    - they'd be **in constant trouble** ("is He safe?"
    … "no, but he's good")

What allows freedom is emotional security, not intellectual… so develop our hearts more than our minds – the Asian Christian who says to Westerners "Your minds have been converted, but not your hearts"

There is no greater moral power or inner strength than to stand before a disordered world, free of its rewards and securities

Imaging learning to swim, then always staying in shallow water

"Our doubts are traitors and make us lose
the good we oft might win, by fearing to attempt"
William Shakespeare (in "Measure for Measure")

"Some men die from shrapnel, some go down in flames,
most people perish inch by inch, playing little games."
Robert Abrahams (in "The Night They Burned Shanghai")

BRIEF HISTORY OF NLF/NLA

After 30 years in Young Life, four years in Bangladesh, and four years on staff of a Presbyterian church, I was encouraged by some who knew me well to start a Leadership Foundation (LF). Although I didn't know what an LF was, I did have a strong background in the urban and cross-cultural world, having lived in six of America's largest cities, plus the four years in Asia. The first year (1989-90) I visited about 75 urban pastors and ministries that gave me a good awareness of who was doing what in the city.

Early on I began meeting regularly with different pastors and ministry leaders, both to encourage and also to respond to their requests for assistance of various sorts – program evaluation, organizational review, vision clarification, etc. Often it was simply a matter of affirmation or a friendly ear. But soon I began to see a number of areas where some specific hands-on involvement could make a difference. List below is a run-down on a number of those specific ventures initiated by NLF, and later NLA.

Holly Park Daycare

The Holly Park Daycare Center, located in a major public housing project in Seattle, was being run poorly and owed the IRS more than $15,000 in unpaid taxes. It became hugely successful after we:

- paid for two studies to determined its viability
- raised $20,000 to keep it going
- arranged a debt repayment plan
- developed a Board of local pastors and others, and
- convinced the ECOM Board to take it over.

Education

ECOM asked us to help their tutoring program of 15 kids. NLF brought on Patti Bylsma as an education consultant, as she had extensive experience in developing tutoring programs. By the end of the year, we had 50 kids being tutored twice a week with 50 volunteers. The next year, we created Tutors' LInc, putting tutoring programs in black churches – 7 churches in the first year and 13 more churches the next year. We were the primary initiator in coalescing a citywide tutor-training program, including most major agencies, such as Catholic Community Services, CAYA, Atlantic Street, and others. Patti wrote a training manual for tutors, which Washington Mutual published and distributed statewide. Two years later, we turned TL over to World Vision, as our intent was to not own or run programs, but to help others succeed. We later contracted with CCS and others in operating their tutoring programs.

Operation Blessing

OB (CBN/700 Club) asked us to become their vehicle for disbursing matching funds and material goods for emergency and special needs of the poor. We have disbursed more than $1 million through 60+ churches and civic agencies. In addition, we have distributed about 5,000 Bibles, about 3,000 blankets each year, and have influenced their procedures nationally for fund distribution.

World Vision/Economic Development

Before World Vision considered moving north from the Los Angeles area, they asked us to help them set up their ministry locally. We created a Board (fairly high profile … George Benson, Seattle City Council Chair; Norm Maleng, King County Pros. Atty: Ron Sims, King County Councilman; Father Mike Ryan, St. James Cathedral; Herb Pfiffner, Executive Director of Union Gospel Mission; and myself). I chaired the Board the first couple years, and we hired a person to set up and run a tutoring program. WV did not want to have the local person on their payroll from a distance, so for the first few years, NLF had WV staff in Seattle, Tacoma, Houston, and Detroit on our payroll – funded of course via WV. Regular contracts were laid out semi-annually.

In a separate program, and using funds from WV, we created a job-development training program in four churches, with hundreds of unemployed finding work – some programs are still going effectively.

Later when WV moved to Federal Way, we entered into an agreement to work collaboratively in urban ministry in the Seattle-Tacoma area.

Tacoma

Early on we were introduced to several urban pastors in Tacoma and began meeting almost weekly with them. Over a period of several years, we participated in planning programs for the Hilltop area, including heading up some long-range planning days. We assisted several churches in their extensive community outreach programs, and in 1993 Ron Detrick joined NLF in Tacoma, where he initiated a variety of outreach ministry opportunities. Later, when I wanted to pass on the baton, Dave Hillis too over NLF, building on Ron's early efforts.

Justice Issues

We participated in monthly meetings with a group of Christian attorneys and judges to look at issues of justice from a biblical perspective. We sponsored several breakfasts and luncheons, which incorporated a large number of other attorneys, and featured speakers such as Washington Supreme Cour Justice Bob Utter, Ray Bakke, and others. NLF arranged for 6 weeks of meetings on various justice issues—e.g., tenant/landlord rights—each in a different black church and led by both black and anglo Christian judges and attorneys.

Leadership Conferences/Consultations

NLF was the convener for a number of conferences that involved men such as Ray Bakke, Tony Campolo, and Jim Wallis, in Seattle, Tacoma, and Portland.

- At a seminar led by Jim Wallis, he expressed publicly his amazement at the mix of those attending – equally divided by Catholics, mainline protestants, and evangelicals.
- We sponsored a 2-day consultation in Portland, having it co-sponsored locally by the Director of the Oregon Ecumenical Council, the director of Portland Evangelical Ministries, and the chair of the African-American Council.
- A 2-day consultation in Seattle with Ray Bakke included the Chief Editor of the Seattle Times, the owner of Fisher media, a school board member, et al.

Youth Ministries/Scholarship Programs

We initiated meetings with youth workers, bringing together the staff of Young Life, Youth for Christ, and directors of youth ministries in large churches. This culminated in a 1-day seminar with more than 500 area youth leaders attending. It featured main speakers and 18 seminars.

We created a scholarship program for minorities, making it possible for several to go to college who otherwise would not have been able to attend. We worked with SPU in their church-related scholarship program, and we created a scholarship fund for urban pastoral education, assisting several through seminary and others in special programs.

Northwest Christian Community Foundation

We were asked to take over as Executive Director of this fledgling foundation. We reconfigured the board, laid out director for future development, and sponsored several seminars with financial and development experts. Then when some men from Oregon came to see what we were doing as they were planning to start their own foundation, we asked them to take over NCCF. It became very successful with almost $10 million in hand.

Coalition for Community Renewal

We were part of two different groups of African-American pastors, including being an officer on one of their boards. Later we began meeting with a group of six black pastors. We met every week for six years and created the CCR and later the CCDevelopment, the latter a non-profit, through which CCR would do economic development. The primary effort of CCD was in seven units of housing, arranged over a period of time that included developing a partnership between two large churches (one urban and one suburban) to build one home together. We also arranged a bank loan for a single mother with 2 kids who had a negative net worth. Promise Keepers asked us to help them develop urban and suburban churches in the area.

Church/Denominational Assistance
- The Billy Graham group asked us to head up their Love-in-Action program for their week in Seattle. During that week and afterwards, we set up meetings with Ray Bakke and other pastors.

- The C&MA asked us for input in their church-planting intentions for Seattle. We took their vision on a 180-degree turn. We help them initiate the creation of the Urban Mission Alliance, which now has multiple staff and ministries on Capital Hill and a new church.
- We assisted the Assembly of God to develop their post-high school training program and helped them create a non-profit organization for that.
- Gethsemane Lutheran asked me to lead their long-range planning efforts, then asked for help to create a non-profit for their dream of building a large downtown high-rise complex for low-income housing. The project became larger than my expertise ($150 million), so we brought in an expert who could carry it forward.

Other Miscellaneous Activities
- Helped initiate the Salem Leadership Foundation
- Laid the groundwork for a NLF satellite in Spokane
- Handled numerous requests for mentoring, including Fuller students in urban evangelism
- Overseas mission involvement meant 2-3 months in Albania, 3 weeks in Turkey, a month in Cuba, and 2 weeks in Bangladesh
- Responded to numerous requests for ministry assistance, including the create of 8-10 non-profit organizations (and helped more to not start)
- Helped the National Association of Street Schools (based in Denver) in developing their ministry, writing templates for their website for schools to copy various procedures, evaluating their schools in four states, and serving on their Board

- Helped create and develop Eagle Wings Ministries, a group that helps people with disabilities in north Puget Sound
- Received an award from Colin Powell in Philadelphia as one of the 1,000 points of light
- Served on more than 12 Boards of Directors, including universities

Much more could be listed, but the above gives an overview of a good bit of what NLF pursued since its inception. Again, our intention was not to own or run our own programs, but rather be a catalyst, as our mission statement said, "to encourage, strengthen and develop leadership for the spiritual and social renewal of the city."

NLF/NLA LETTERS

In the process of writing these memoirs, several encouraged me to include some of the monthly letters I wrote in previous years. This part of the appendix provides copies of 18 of those letters.

NORTHWEST LEADERSHIP FOUNDATION

October 1994

"And the little people are being encouraged." Jesus

From my current reading in chapter 11 in Matthew's gospel, I am again challenged out of my socks by the intriguing insights from Dale Bruner's commentary.

John the Baptist had baptized Jesus, the Messiah-to-be. What in the world is he doing in prison, he wonders. Certainly a Messiah would have chosen followers with better credentials. And his Messiah-like miracles would have been performed in the capital (Jerusalem), not "in northern Idaho" (Galilee). Jesus does not seem sufficiently messianic. So John sends word: "Are you really The One or not?"

Jesus replies with this simple statement:

> "Tell John the things that you are hearing and seeing: the blind see again and the lame are walking; lepers are cleansed and the deaf hear; the dead are being raised, **and the little people are being encouraged**." (One translation gives this last phrase as "and the wretched of the earth learn that God is on their side.")

Bruner points out that commentators are intrigued by Jesus putting at the end of his list the apparent climax what most of us would consider the least impressive of the things he did. Standing next to "the dead are being raised", this good news to the poor comes as anticlimax. Surely a word to the poor cannot compare with raising the dead.

But Jesus counts among his best work the encouraging Word to the down, the grief-stricken, the poor, the little people. "Jesus intends to summarize the Sermon on the Mount, which begins 'Blessed are the poor in spirit.'" And, in Bruner's comments on this first Beatitude, he points out poignantly that the Hebrew *anawin,* "poor", were "those who were **poor and crushed as a result**... those who **feel** their poverty, who **suffer** their poverty, and so **cry out to heaven**. In his opening words, Jesus puts himself on the side of the wretched of the earth."

> "So the Sermon on the Mount is meant to be an encouraging message to little people, and his word here to John is that even raising the dead did not rival renewing the living. The Sermon on the Mount is the *Magna Carta* of the little people, it is the best news for common men and women because it tells them how they are regarded and how to live—and why. It raises from the dead in its own way: it raises the little into big, broad, and humane life, the common into an uncommon life, the insignificant into a life with new meaning. Give life to the dead is something; but giving the living a way to live is something, too."

Our commitment to NLF is to build bridges—connecting the Christian community with those who have little hope, who see no future, who struggle to make it every day—to somehow help the Church carry out the heart of Jesus. So that **the little people are being encouraged.**

It takes time, patience, wisdom, but we're seeing it happen. Thanx for your part!

Bud Bylsma

March 1995

Dear Friends,

Not infrequently I become involved in helping someone sort out his or her calling and ministry. Last year we helped 4 or 5 individuals start non-profit ministries, but we also helped as many or more to **not** start. Yesterday was one of the latter, as a gentleman sat sharing his dreams and desires, but it finally became obvious to him that he was not equipped to initiate what he thought was a "calling."

There's a fine line between that which God asks us to do and our own self-interests. I face that almost every day. Frederick Buechner, in his book <u>Wishful Thinking: A Theological ABC,</u> gave what I thought were some beautiful thoughts on this, and which I pass on:

> *There are all kinds of voices calling you to all different kinds of work, and the problem is to find out which is the voice of God rather than of society, say, or the Superego, or Self-interest. By and large a good rule for finding out is this: The kind of work God usually calls you to is the kind of work*
>
> A. *that you need to do, and*
> B. *that the world most needs to have done.*
>
> *If you really get a kick out of your work, you've presumably met requirement (A), but if your work is writing TV deodorant commercials, the chances are you've missed requirement (B). On the other hand, if your work is being a doctor in a leper colony, you have probably met requirement (B), but if most of*

*the time you're bored and depressed by it, the chances are you
have not only bypassed (A) but probably aren't helping your
patients much either!*

> *Neither the hair shirt nor the soft berth will do. The
> place Gods calls you is the place where your deep
> gladness and the world's deep hunger meet.*

Our desire in NLF is that we will be joyous as we seek to care
about the city. Please pray this month for:

1. approval of a grant proposal of $175,000 submitted for
   housing development (we just got word of approval of a
   $25,000 interest-free loan!)

2. the urban/suburban church partnerships to be developing
   in the building of homes.

So many good things are happening --- thanx for your role in
our lives and ministry.

Bud Bylsma

September 1995

> ### CONGRUENCE "Coinciding exactly
> when superimposed" (Webster)

"The Gospel came not in word only ..." Paul

Congruence—when words and actions match—when life and lip correspond. The great missiologist Leslie Newbigen says:

> *The word without the deep is hollow*
> *The deed without the word is dumb.*

The Church today can't say she cares about the city and stay uninvolved. Love, by its very nature, always reaches out – **touches**. I'm impressed with a beautify story by Max DuPree in his book, <u>Leadership Jazz</u>, about the birth of his granddaughter:

> *Esther my wife and I have a granddaughter named Zoe, the Greek word for life. She was born prematurely and weighed one pound, seven ounces, so small that my wedding ring could slide up her arm to her should. The neonatologist who first examined her told us that she had a five to ten percent chance of living three days. When Esther and I scrubbed up for our first visit and saw Zoe in her isolette in the neonatal intensive care unit, she had two IVs in her navel, one in her foot, a monitor tube and a feeding tube in her mouth.*

> *To complicate matters, Zoe's biological father had jumped ship the month before Zoe was born. Realizing this, a wise and caring nurse named Ruth gave me my instructions. "For the next several months, at least, you are the surrogate father. I*

want you to come to the hospital every day to visit Zoe, and when you come, I would like you to rub her body and her legs and arms with the tip of your finger. While you are caressing her, you should tell her over and over how much you love her, because she has to be able to connect your voice to your touch.

Ruth was doing exactly the right thing on Zoe's behalf (and of course on my behalf as well). And without realizing it, she was giving me one of the best possible descriptions of the work of a leader. At the core of becoming a leader is the need always to connect one's voice with one's touch.

We in NLF are committed to having a strong, felt presence in the city, connecting word with touch. And we believe that God is using us to help the Church do the same, with some beautiful urban/suburban partnerships developing. An offer has been submitted by the 6-pastor Coalition to purchase the 3 acres for low-income housing, and we'll know the outcome within a week. Please continue to pray re this.

Bud Bylsma

July 1996

> *"If we fail in the city, it will become*
> *a cesspool." D. L. Moody*

Failure. So many children growing up in urban America feel a lack of confidence and self-esteem, a sense of inadequacy. Most of today's role models do not provide positive images. The school drop-out rate continues to soar. Billions of dollars pour into urban programs, and yet our urban communities struggle to survive.

We in NLF are among those who believe the answer to our city's needs is not from the outside, but from those who live there. Like most others, not everything we do succeeds. But we like our batting average. And perhaps that's because our commitment is to **persons** more than programs, to see individuals in **potential**, not present performance.

Those who fail early are in some good company.

Didn't Finish Grade School	Didn't Finish High School	Had a Learning Disability
Mark Twain	George Gershwin	Tom Cruise
Charles Dickens	Will Rogers	Woodrow Wilson
Claude Monet	Peter Jennings	Nelson Rockefeller
	both Wright brothers	Leonardo da Vinci

- **Babe Ruth** his 714 home runs but **struck out 1,330 times**.
- Walt Disney was fired by a newspaper editor because "**he had no good ideas**."

- An executive dismissed **Fred Astaire** with the opinion "Can't act... can't sing... balding... **can dance a little**."
- **Abraham Lincoln** began the Blackhawk War as a captain, but **ended the war as a Private.**

The Gospel is **"with a hope and a future,"** and our commitment in NLF is to see "beauty from ashes," to see leadership emerge from within the city that will cause the Church to be both a sign and an agent of God's kingdom – where Christ is more loved and known than ever before. Northwest Leadership Foundation has its focus on just that – leadership – as we seek to discover those who have the potential in spite of the present.

Bud Bylsma

September 1996

This past month I was interviewed twice on a radio program whose focus is leadership. In the second interview, I was asked "what are the essential ingredients for being a leader in the city?" Here was my spontaneous response.

1. **Vision**... an eye for possibilities, **seeing what can be** more than what is. "Faith is like a crouching lion, waiting for what it knows will come by." I believe vision is the **gift of faith** – not only seeing what can be but how to get there, and then involving others to make it happen.

2. **Must love the city**... an effective Christian leader will love not only the people but the place, and see the city through biblical eyes. God intends the city to be a place that provides for the well-being of its people. The greatest book in the Old Testament on evangelism, Jonah, ends with the last verse showing God's incredible care for that city.

3. **Risk**... willing to "color outside the lines," venture into uncharted waters. And secure enough to be free to fail. The city is not a place for the faint of heart. In the litany of the heroes of faith in Hebrews 11, we mostly focus on that first large group and easily forget those mentioned from verse 35 on who were "tortured... flogged, imprisoned, stoned, sawed in two, death by the sword... destitute, persecuted" etc. Faith isn't what rescues us, but what **guides** us.

4. **Learning and persistence**... real change doesn't come quickly, and it is imperative to be there as a **learner**, listening, discovering that we may have more to learn than

to give, that those different from ourselves actually enrich our lives.

5. Compassion… which means to **suffer with**. That means **not reaching** down but **going** down. It means being the "servant leader," connecting with their brokenness, not our strengths. Empowering them, "showing them **their** riches, not our own" (Paschal). It was the **Pharisee** who prayed, "I thank you that I am not like other men." But Jesus became one **like** us.

Much more was and could be said than the above, and perhaps we will elaborate in months ahead. But our prayer is that at least these will be the characteristics of us as NLF—loving the city, learning, compassionate, risking, and with a real vision for what can be—God's presence being felt and seen more than ever.

Bud Bylsma

March 1997

The Issue Isn't Welfare Reform. It's Poverty

So reads the heading on the cover of the current "SOJOURNERS" Magazine, referring to one of the most controversial issues of our day. Might this be a grand opportunity for the Church to take the lead in fulfilling its mandate as the primary source of care for the less advantaged?

So much is presumed and written about the poor. I thought it would be of interest to point out some common myths about "the poor", as taken from a recent Washington D.C. bulletin:

MYTH 1: *The majority of the poor live in inner city neighborhoods.*

FACT: Less than half the poor (42%) live in central city areas, while 36% live in the suburbs and 22% live outside metropolitan areas.

MYTH 2: *People are poor because they do not want to work.*

FACT: Half of the poor are in traditional working ages of 18 to 65; the other half are children and the elderly. About 30% of the working-age poor do not work— many cannot work because of a reported disability or because they care for family members.

MYTH 3: *The vast majority of the poor are African-American or Hispanic.*

FACT: Non-Hispanic whites make up the largest number of persons in poverty.

MYTH 4: *The poor live off government welfare.*

FACT: Welfare accounts for about 25% of the income of poor adults. Nearly half the income they receive comes from wages or other work-related activity.

MYTH 5: *Poor families are trapped in a cycle of poverty that few escape.*

FACT: Only 12% of the poor remain in poverty for 5 or more consecutive years.

MYTH 6: *Welfare programs for the poor are straining the government.*

FACT: Social assistance programs for low-income families and individuals accounted for 14% of projected federal expenditures in 1996. A much larger share of the budget (43%) goes to other types of social assistance, such as Social Security and Medicare, which mainly go to middle-class Americans, not the poor.

The major commitment of NLF is to **help the poor discover their riches,** to create a future they never imagined possible. And it's happening. This week a wonderful family whose net worth was $0 is moving into a **new** home. PTL! And we'll have at least 10 each year. Our efforts in assisting the urban church toward self-development are seeing some very tangible results. Thanx for your support in making all this possible.

Yours and His,

Bud Bylsma

NORTHWEST LEADERSHIP ASSOCIATES

September 2001

I had started writing this month's letter about the city, when "The City" got devastated on September 11. Incredible horror. Within 24 hours half a dozen calls and emails came, asking for understanding of what was going on. It seems that almost all of us feel violated and vulnerable – huge devastation to the American psyche. I'm certainly no expert and not sure that any of us rational persons can grasp the irrational, but at the expense of maybe saying the obvious, here are some random thoughts.

There are obviously a number of related issues at work here – the Arab/Israeli antagonism, (which, in my opinion, is irresolvable) – the double-bind in which we find ourselves, supporting Israel while needing Arab oil – the bind the Saudis are in, wanting Western $ from oil, but Muslim in heart (and the home of Mecca and Medina, the 2 most holy Islamic sites) – the hatred of bin Laden, et al, for Saudi monarchy for allowing US troop presence, since where Mohammed lived is sacred land and should be off limits to non-Muslims – the Saddam/Iraq situation, where Arabs feel sanctions have mostly hurt children – the rich/poor disparity – etc.

Underlying everything, there is a difference in the East and West and how we function. We in the West are Greek, the result of Hellenistic, rational thought; the Eastern mind is Hebrew and operates supra-rationally, that is, outside the rational. They operate much more from the gut. "As a man thinks in his **heart**, so is he" – that's Eastern. We think with our **heads**, our minds – that's Western. That's one of the primary differences (incidentally, the African-American culture is Eastern, third-world, and they, too, respond more viscerally than from the head). So the question "how could anyone do this?" is a logical question, but irrelevant to the ethos of passion.

And so a growing number of Islamic fundamentalists, who see America as the Great Satan – who are honored in martyrdom – whose logic is passion – who see no difference of soldier or civilian – have absolutely no qualms about their jihad (holy war). The Muslim religion does not differentiate between religion, economics, politics, etc. All of the West is viewed as Christian, and the Christian West has brought to them morals and values which they consider abhorrent, especially as influencing their children. When Charlton Heston was in Dhaka to do a film (and Patti and I had a private dinner with him and his family), he told a five-star hotel audience of the media that "the greatest contribution America has given to Bangladesh is it's movie industry." I could hardly believe it, aware that there were more than 500 porn shops in Dhaka, with mostly western movies. It is this sort of thing that drives the Muslim fundamentalist to do what he is doing – this, and then magnified by the Israeli and oil and rich/poor issues.

Reluctantly perhaps, I add that I rather think their victory in NY will no doubt encourage other dissidents from a variety of locations. I'm inclined to think that some have seen our presumed invincibility as penetrable, which may only be their encouragement. Our safe harbors may not be as safe as had previously thought, and might it be true, as some are saying, that our way of life may be significantly altered in the future.

I choose not to speculate on the prophetic, but do trust that as Christians we will be attuned to hear what God has to say to us, individually and as a nation. Do we fear the future? Or embrace it? The occasional pang I've felt this past year, watching our small retirement fund dwindle – and now what? Where is my ultimate trust, really?

As ever, (almost)

Bud Bylsma

May 2002

HIDING IN THE LIGHT

In our growing up years, most of us no doubt had numerous episodes of being **afraid of the dark**. How I remember many times as a young boy, reluctant to walk a certain path at night, simply because of the "boogey-man." Looking back on it, I realized the fears were quite unfounded – those were really days of being quite safe, even alone during the dark nights.

A friend told of being on a medical mission at an orphanage in Beirut, housing about 200 children, but the ravages of war had increased the number to more than 2000. Making his way down rickety stairs with almost no light, he tripped over a lump of something in the hallway – how rude that they would not keep the hall clear. When a light shone, the "lump" turned out to be a 14-year-old boy whose body was twisted and misshapen by what he later learned was muscular dystrophy. With chagrin, he simply apologized.

How easy it is to be afraid of invading the dark places because of "night blindness." Isaiah says "Justice is far from us, and righteousness does not reach us… we look for light, but all is darkness; for brightness, but we walk in deep shadows." How many people in our cities live like this – blind, groping and stumbling – hungry, lonely, shivering, because of injustice. How quickly we forget what it's like in the dark. And how easy it is to hide in the light.

I was reared to avoid evil, not how to overcome it – not to associate with the world, in order to stay pure. So avoid the dark. But Paul was called to the darkness of immoral Corinth, corrupt Rome, and the dank prison of Philippi. On one occasion he said "now I go... not knowing what will happen there."

The struggle for us as God's people is to walk in the light, and at the same time keep moving into the shadows. And when our eyes have adjusted to the dark through constant exposure, we discover ways to see lumps in the dark places as challenges, not obstacles.

On speaking occasionally to students in the past who were considering missions, I used to cite the quote on the wall of the Coast Guard in Massachusetts – **"You must go out... you don't have to come back."** I am increasingly aware that the adventure of living out Christ's life in today's world may mean more association among darkness than the comfort of hiding in the light. As was said of Aslan: **"Is he safe?" "No, but he's good."**

Bud Bylsma

February 2003

Meet Me On The Patio

The above phrase has been ringing in my mind on frequent occasions this past month, so I decided to follow my heart and write about it. It's the title of a book by Karl Olsson, former president of North Park College and Seminary in Chicago, and the diagram on the next page (as best as I remember) was what gave the book its title. I make various comments of my own here, having given away the book many years ago.

The diagram is like 2 side-by-side apartments, each representing us as two individuals, and **connected** by a **common ground** floor. This ground floor represents our **common humanity**, where all have the same basic needs, passions, passages, etc. The balcony on each floor is that from which we connect and communicate with others. On the first floor is our personhood, that which makes each of us different from one another. We then explore our **talents**, which with x amount of training develop into **skills**. As those skills are developed, we are able to move into **tasks** and **roles**, which, when more fully developed, give us **status**, as we climb the ladder. And for a few, that expertise may even lead to **preeminence** – head of major institutions, etc.

Our tendency is to relate from the balcony to others who are on the same level, or above us – where it's most comfortable – most self-affirming, ego fulfilling. When from our balcony we look at another significantly above us, we tend to **pedestal** that person. Conversely, when we look at another somewhat below us, we tend to **patronize**. But in each case, we rarely connect on a deeper personal level, relating superficially on our various levels of role or status, waving from one balcony to another – we forget that real connectedness is at the common ground level.

When God chose to communicate and relate to us, he set aside all human levels, identifying and connecting with us on the **lowest level**, our **common humanity**. The man in the Temple, thumping his chest, says "I thank God I am not like all the others." **But Jesus became *like* all the others** – affirming us in our common humanity, not our giftedness.

Meeting on the patio may be like someone has said of purgatory – it's painful, but a struggle that is taking us somewhere. It seems to me that if suburbia is going to impact the urban setting, there will need to be much more time meeting on the patio – perhaps purgatorially painful, but eventually we might get somewhere.

Bud Bylsma

Relationship Model

Karl Olsson (<u>Meet Me On The Patio</u>, 1977)

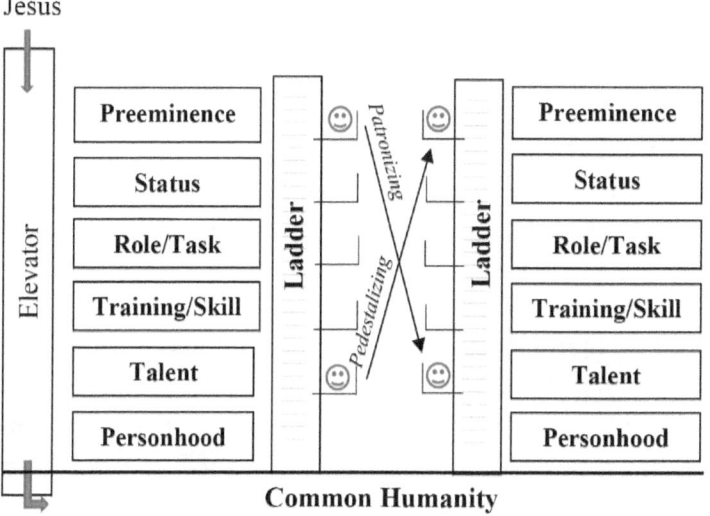

March 2003

Relief vs Development

Last year a branch of the 700 Club, Operation Blessing, asked me to write several short papers on 'development', and, liking what I wrote for the first one, plan to publish it. A couple of folks who saw it suggested that I send it to my mailing list, so that's what I submit for this month's missive. I certainly do not consider myself an expert in this comparatively new and rather complex field of development, but submit in a rather elementary way what I have learned.

Here on the local scene, Patti returned two weeks ago from her month in Cuba. It was not an easy time for her, and her living conditions were at times somewhat less than comfortable, but she felt it was very good in the teaching of English to several groups. She was in Havana for the first 3 weeks, and then a week and a half in Pinar del Rio where she was able to be with her brother, and also with many of those from the classes we taught at the seminary a year ago. We feel very good about being able to be of assistance to our friends in Cuba, not only in the English teaching but also in helping in a variety of ways to assist the church leadership there. In a country where relief would be most welcome almost everywhere, our desire is for much more, real development.

Well, below is the paper as presented to the 700 Club.

Most cordially,

Bud Bylsma

* * * * * * * * * *

The Discipline of Development

Our task is to delineate between **relief** and **development**, two very different approaches in addressing human need. Development is much more elusive than relief, since it is long-term in its efforts, and thus far more elusive. Providing relief gives the **giver** immediate gratification, as one sees a person relieved from an immediate need – food? clothing? shelter? medical? However, nothing has changed toward having that person no longer in need of a "hand-out." As the old proverb states, development teaches how to fish, not just giving a fish – a long arduous process.

In the broad area of development, there are two different components – community development vs. personal, or individual development. The former must involve group process—a number of people and/or agencies who determine to create change and renewal of an entire community. However, development in the life of an individual can be accomplished one-on-one, although usually a very long process. That's because there needs to be a total reversal of that person's own self-perception, self-worth, self-esteem, self-image. Ultimately genuine development results in the transformation of a person, he/she being able to have totally new ability to become fully responsible for their own future.

Here are a few general definitions of development:
  - a conscientization process by which a person is awakened to opportunities within their reach
  - uplift of spirit – awareness of one's own gifts and power

- a release from forces holding one down
- ability to make one's own decisions, act on one's own behalf
- increased initiative and control over one's own destiny
- full self-reliance.

The starting point for development must be from within the person him/her self. In relief, we "help" another, give to the other. However, in development **we are not able to "develop" another – one can only develop him/her self**. In my role, I do not give to another that which I possess – I help the other discover **that which they already own.** As the renowned Blaise Pascal said, "**he showed us our riches, not his own.**" So the starting point is within myself, to see that I do not have the answers to that person's real need, but rather seeing my responsibility was to help the one toward discovering their own "riches."

People are not poor because they have no money – they are poor because they have no power, have few choices in many areas of life. But the **greatest poverty is in having nothing to give.** That person functions needing to receive from whomever is willing to give – with their hand out – so demeaning, debilitating, dehumanizing to the human spirit.

So there are two major steps in personal development, both huge. Step one is to **"show them their riches,"** as Pascal said. That is such a huge step because it involves two different agendas. One, it's long-term (and we Americans want quick results), and two, it means **my stepping down from my role of "giver"** to enter into **his/her** world. Jesus used the term compassion rarely, for good reason – it is much deeper than "love." In Latin it's "*cum pati*" – **to suffer with,** to have the bowels yearn. That means

***going* down, not *reaching* down.** And of course that's exactly what Jesus did (Phil. 2:5-8). Genuine development of a person will almost never occur without having one person enter into the heart, the hurt and the pain of another. And that takes a huge amount of time and patience and humility.

Step two follows after I helped that person discover their own giftedness. Now I put myself in the position of **receiving from that one**, who has now moved from a "receiver" to a giver. Which is what Jesus did in John 4, when he went **down** to Samaria, to the lowest of society. In effect he said to the woman at the well **"you have something I need** ... would you give me some water?" Jesus first put her, alone and a virtual outcast, in touch with something she had to give – having put himself in the position to receive from her. And her whole life was changed, where she felt confident enough to declare to a whole village her own vulnerability. Jesus had empowered her. Development, the transformation from "I am worth nothing" to an outpouring of one's own spirit. (For me, it's the greatest miracle in the N.T. – 3 years of psychoanalysis in 5 minutes.)

In Psalm 18:35, David expresses development beautifully in what could seem an obscure passage, when he says to God, **"You stoop down to make me great."** (See also v. 16) The Incarnation still goes on – our stooping down to make others significant, to lift them up. Cost? Of course! But the privilege is ours, as we emulate our Lord Jesus in the ministry of compassion of lifting up others.

April 2003

Sitting in the Ashes

Last month I wrote re individual 'development' and the difficulty of really making that happen. This month I continue in that vein – quoting in full a previous article by Bruce Knofel, the Executive Director of Bridge Ministries for Disability Concerns – a 'cadillac' ministry. He writes (emphasis added):

"In our staff meeting yesterday we were reflecting on some of the difficult issues the people we serve are facing. We particularly reflected on the emotional struggle being faced by some of our people who are recently disabled. They feel the emotional pain of grief and loss as they recognize that some of their hopes and dreams will never be fulfilled because of their disability. This is real pain. Then Diane, one of our volunteer staff who herself deals with a life changing disability, made an observation that really rang true to us. She said, **'In our communities, it does not seem like there is a place for suffering that does not go away.'**

"Many of us involved in helping others, either as professionals or as volunteers, want to see people 'fixed.' **What are we to do when the suffering does not go away?** As we asked ourselves this question during the staff meeting, Jeannine said, **'We need to sit in the ashes with our people.'** Basically Jeannine was challenging us not to try and 'fix' those who are suffering, but instead **to be present with them in their suffering.** 'Sitting in the ashes' means to **take time to hear the feelings of pain, sadness, grief,** that are being expressed and to acknowledge the feelings.

By doing this we give people a safe place to face their pain and to journey through it. Our supportive listening creates space within a person that **sets them free to find the healing and hope that can be theirs.** It is a paradox that by not trying to 'fix' someone we give them the space they need to find 'healing' for themselves.

"Speaking recently at a luncheon, one of those attending came up to us and shared that her son had a spinal cord injury many years ago. He was left quadriplegic from the accident. She said over the years he has been asked to write letters to others who have had a similar accident 'to make them feel better.' She said **'you can't make them feel better, you can only acknowledge their pain and loss.'**

"It may sound strange to say this, but it is such a privilege to 'sit in the ashes' with others. There is something sacred and holy about being in that place with others because it affirms and celebrates the worth and value of a person. There is something rich and valuable within us that can never be broken or lost. It is such a reward to see beyond the disability to the person and their worth and value that grows out of the ashes."

In being a small part of both Bridge Ministries and Eagle Wings Ministries, both ministering to those with disabilities, I have been much the richer.

As ever,

Bud Bylsma

May 2004

Letters to the Editor

How grateful I am for the occasional note from some of you, expressing your thoughts regarding my letters. You have been most encouraging… well, for the most part. A lengthy response came recently to my February letter on *South of the Border*, in which I alluded to those coming across from our neighbor to the south, many being illegal.

The gist of the letter was decrying the "outsourced" of U.S. firms, and that if they come, they "should come here legally, learn English, and become a citizen…," and more.

Obviously the above refers to our economy and politics, and having people 'doing what's right'. The only reason I chose to comment on this was the lingering thoughts that came to me regarding **culture and the Gospel**. And as I state in that Feb. letter, the biblical mandate is to **"not mistreat the alien"**, which of course meant not just their own, but the 'uninvited' Gentile… who is the neighbor.

How difficult it can be to delineate that which is biblical from that which is cultural. Patti and I have struggled with that for years, and confess that our lifestyle is more cultural than biblical. I'll pass on here quotes from a variety of people on this subject, most of which are a bit disquieting.

Jim Wallis, founder/director of the *Sojourners* magazine and their community in Wash., D.C.:

"The Gospel is an offense to every culture.
The *offense* of the Gospel is in its *discontinuity* with the world.
The *power* of the Gospel is in the *JOY* amid that discontinuity."

George Will, nationally known writer/editor: "The success of a society is more apt to be determined by the **culture** of the society than by the **politics** of it. And its politics can have a deleterious effect on that culture."

Cotton Mather, son of Increase Mather, early Harvard President: **"Religion brought forth prosperity, and the daughter destroyed the mother."**

Newsweek magazine: **"The top 20% owns 80%** of all that can be privately owned in the U.S., **while the bottom 25% owns 0**... the Church has identified with the dominant value system of our culture."

Lesslie Newbigin, world-renowned missiologist: "This pagan western culture has penetrated into every other culture in the world and threatens to destabilize them all." (1984)

Walter Brueggemann, author: "The contemporary American church is so largely enculturated to the American ethos of consumerism that it has little power to believe or to act."

Obviously there are no simple answers to the above, but I would invite your response.

Yours and His,

Bud Bylsma

January 2007

"You begin to die the moment your memories are greater than your dreams"
Howard Hendricks

So what's ahead for us in 2007? I confess I don't really know, as there are a number of different areas of involvement in which I find myself. Several to date have not materialized, but others have done well, such as a health clinic for children from poor families. Two and three years ago they had a total of almost a $100,000 shortfall… we ended 2006 with more than $100,000 in the bank.

So while I'm not at all sure of what this year holds, I like what Erich Fromm says:

> *"To hope means to be ready at every moment*
> *for that which is not yet born, and yet not become desperate*
> *if there is no birth in our lifetime."*

In our two years here, we've been learning the city, looking for those places where seed-planting might take effect. But the wonderful thing is the sense of not having to 'succeed'. I'm not even sure what that would look like. So much is "not yet", and who knows what our meager efforts may show down the road. I love the way the martyred Oscar Romero said it:

> *"It helps, now and then, to step back and take the long. The*
> *Kingdom is not only beyond our efforts, it is even beyond our*
> *vision. We accomplish in our lifetime only a tiny fraction of*
> *the magnificent enterprise that is God's work. Nothing we do*

is complete, which is another way of saying that the Kingdom always lies beyond us.

No statement says all that should be said. No prayer fully expresses our faith. No program accomplishes the Church's mission. No set of goals and objectives includes everything.

This is what we are about. We plant the seeds that one day will grow. We water seeds already planted, know that they hold future promise. We lay foundations that will need further development. We provide yeast that produces effects far beyond our capabilities.

We cannot do everything and there is a sense of liberation in realizing that. This enables us to do something and do it very well. It may be incomplete, but it is a beginning, a step along the way, an opportunity for the Lord's grace to enter and do the rest.

We may never see the end results, but that is the difference between the master builder and the worker. We are workers, not master builders, ministers, not messiahs. We are prophets of a future that is not our own. AMEN."

My prayer is that *"we will plant seeds that one day will grow."* And hopefully we can relax in knowing that we don't have to see the end result… *"a future that is not our own."*

Yours for a blessed new year,

Bud Bylsma

April 2007

"If you want justice, change the laws"
Esther

Queen Esther? Well, not exactly... but close.

The above was a statement in court, from a judge who had been confronted by a minister asking about his decisions. Dr. Bill Leslie, minister of Chicago's LaSalle Street Church, had developed a 357-unit housing complex in that city's poorest community (5 churches had invested $1,000 each, and HUD contributed $11 million... now a national model). So he was definitely interested in low-income housing.

Since a good percentage of housing for low-income persons is run by absentee landlords, it is generally known that frequently those houses are rundown and/or greatly inadequate. That was Bill's concern, as case after case in court on tenant/landlord rights was being ruled in favor of the landlord. He approached the bench — *"Your honor, every case is ruled in favor of the landlord. Where is the justice in this court?"*

The judge's terse but incisive response — *"Dr. Leslie, you need to understand one thing – this is not a court of justice, this is a court of law. If you want justice, change the laws."*

Corporate injustice is at least as old as Haman and King Xerxes, who had decreed that all Jews would be killed. So the orphan girl, Esther, ran for Miss Persia... won the beauty contest... married the king... and **got him to change the law**. Innovative and effective. **Wilberforce did it, too!**

As Ray Bakke says, "There are two verses in the Bible on the virgin birth… I'd believe it if there was only one. There are more than 1,000 verses on the poor and oppressed, **67 on injustice toward the poor."** (Have you ever heard one sermon on the latter?) The O.T. word "*shalom*" essentially means **"*a just peace.*"** God told Jeremiah to "*seek the welfare (shalom) of the city, for in its welfare is yours also.*" (And that was **Babylon!**) Huge efforts are being given by 'the Church' toward at least a couple of major social issues… is this biblical issue worthy of similar attention?

I've been invited to participate in efforts to bring together disparate ethnic groups. As I've said earlier, re a city with little connectedness… can it happen? Pray that God will give wisdom.

Bud Bylsma

May 2007

Life from the Center

For the last couple of years Patti and I have been in a bi-weekly book discussion group, one of the members being a college professor. Recently he told of a conversation among a group of colleagues, with the question posed as to what would be the most important question you would ask of students in your class. Understandably, most of the responses focused around the subject matter of their respective disciplines.

After some thought, I suggested that the most important question any of us might ask of ourselves could have to do with the subject of Victor Frankl's old book, **Man's Search for Meaning**... what is the basic meaning of life? Of **my** life? After more reflection on this, I thought... might there be one even more bottom-line question for any of us, and of which I should ask myself... what is my **center**? That is, what is at the very core of my life which gives meaning as to who I am, and a rationale for all I do? What drives me... gives **focus**... **cohesion**... **meaning** to my very existence... that which influences every area of my life?

Years ago Dr. Kerr, the Chancellor of the huge University of California systems, made the comment that the institution should not be called a University, but a Multiversity, since the only unifying factor was the administration. The center was not the academics, but the administration.

So what is the unifying factor in our lives… that which helps define who we are, and what we do, out from which all of life flows… vocation, family, etc.… am I a **multi**… or **uni** person?

On the next page are two diagrams, illustrating the many-sided areas of life. One shows life more compartmentalized, where I may be a different person at different times, and where there may be little or no inter-relatedness to other areas. The center may be any one of those… that which has most of my time and attention. The other depicts how all of life is inter-related, and where **the Center impacts every area**… we're the same person in each, with Christ as the influencing factor in every area of life.

The late Dr. Richard Halvorsen said, "A man becomes like what he thinks about all day long." Karl Barth was probably the greatest theologian of the 20th century, and when he was on the cover of TIME magazine, they said of him, **"Karl Barth is a Christ-intoxicated man."** Wow! Can any comment be greater of any person? **A uni man.** You? Me?

Bud Bylsma

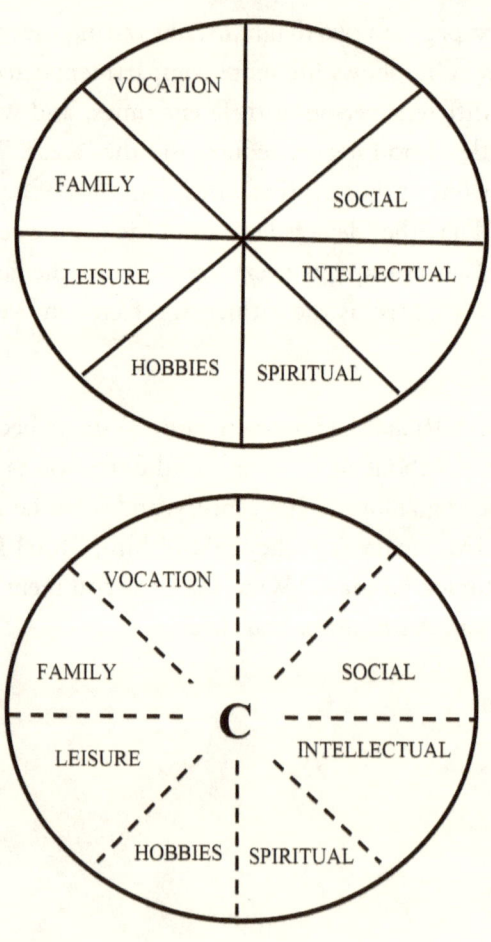

December 2007 *(Christmas letter printed on red paper)*

A Cemetery Tour – Then A Birth

Most of my life I read Scripture through my middle-class bifocals… so limiting, I discovered, in not seeing so many cultural implications. **Matthew 1:1-17** was rather irrelevant… "so and so begat so and so, who begat…" But then the gift of our years in Bangladesh. In the Asian/Eastern culture, one's identity is authenticated via male heritage… **one's father**. So Eastern thinking about this passage would be that Jesus must have been **really important**… this fathers are named all the way back to Abraham.

But the truly amazing thing in the Matthew account is that, aside from Mary, **4 women** are mentioned in these verses. Women were virtually **never** mentioned in a royal family tree. Yet even **more amazing** is the **sort** of women mentioned… all a part of Jesus' 'tree.'

Tamar – resorted to trickery in acting as a **prostitute** to seduce her **father-in-law, Judah** (Jesus, the Lion of the tribe Judah)

Rahab – a **Canaanite (foreigner) harlot**… the mother of Boaz, David's great-grandfather

Ruth – a **Moabite (foreigner)** and wife of Boaz, David's great-grandmother

Bathsheba – not mentioned by name, but as "wife of Uriah," the **Hittite**

Jesus' bloodline – women of **scandal… sinners… foreigners.**

God chose to choreograph into the very life of Jesus those scandalous bloodlines of many nations, smashing ethnocentrism and racism, so that **the blood which Jesus shed *for* the world would be from the blood *of* the world.** (And how many children age 2 and under died for Jesus before he died for them?) We've gone upscale and made the birth scene rather antiseptic, but life and Scripture, as seen from the 'underside' gives perspective from a wider lens.

Then Matthew, in **beginning** with the nations, also **ends** with the nations, in that 'Great Commission.' So as Patti and I enjoy the celebration of Jesus' birth, we also, like the end of Matthew, wonder if in our 'ending years' God is encouraging us toward 'the nations.' We sense a movement in that direction, **Africa** in particular, where the needs are so great. And we are really rather excited about some possibilities... just not sure of all the specifics at this time. So please pray with us as we seek clarity and direction... we'll keep you posted.

A blessed Christmas and opportunity-filled New Year to each of you.

Bud Bylsma

April 2008

The Power of the Resurrection

We celebrated Easter early this year... Holy Week, the focal point of all Christianity... the **Cross** and the **Resurrection**. It seems to me there are two kinds of power... that of the **atom** ...and that of **leaven**.

Both are valid, both effective... one highly visible, the other almost imperceptible. So perhaps a question might be... what sort of power will make Christ and His presence most strongly felt and **visible in the city**?

A 'crusade' can influence many lives—valid, highly visible, effective in targeted areas. But in working closely with the Billy Graham team in the '90's, they concurred that their efforts have been very limited in touching the core of a city... the underclass, the blue-collar, the ethnic minority, the less-advantaged. Might it be that **leaven** speaks more strongly to a city than the atom?

Jesus said "I have **power** to lay down my life, I have **power** to take it up..." Apparently Jesus used his power to lay down his life, but did **not** use his power to raise it up. The book of Acts speaks repeatedly of "**God**, who raised up Jesus from the dead"... and Paul says in Phil. 2 that Jesus 'emptied' himself, and "therefore **God** has highly exalted him." Jesus' power was shown sacrificially giving his life **for others**.

Revelation 5 speaks of the unopened scroll... "I wept and wept, because no one was found worthy to open the scroll..." Then, "do not weep... the **Lion**... is able... then I saw a **Lamb**, looking as if it had been slain... 'you are worthy... because you were slain.'" The Lion is never referred to again, only the Lamb... worthy **because he became the Lamb**.

Might Resurrection power actually be in the **power to die**? Does the Church today have the power to lay down its life for the sake of the city... for those with whom Jesus connected... can it say **"this is Jesus body, broken for you?"** If not, do we have a message? How will the Gospel be seen and felt in the city, that catch-basin of people in need? How might the Church be in touch with the needy... quietly, imperceptibly, **leaven-like**... that the **power** of Christ will be seen?

It is said that the church of tomorrow will be the '**missional** church'... the church for 'others'... where compassion and caring about the 'have-nots' is a signature. Yours?

Bud Bylsma

December 2003 *(Christmas letter printed on red paper)*

Some thoughts from the saints of yesterday...

God's becoming human
  Is not an idyll,
  It is a scandal!
  God meets us
In the lowliness of a child.
  (Saint Jerome)

The human race was made
  in God's likeness
but, since we lost that form
God took our human likeness
this night, when He was born.
  (Andreas Gryphius)

If God became one of us in Jesus, that is surely something that we can never value highly enough. We can place all our human hopes on him. If Jesus is at the same time both God and our brother, then I should never know fear again. *(Carlo Carretto)*

God is the Lord
and he appeared to us,
He came, not in the form of God,
so that he would not frighten the weak,
but in the form of a servant,
so that he could lead the enslaved to freedom.
Is there anyone
who is so weary,
or so ungrateful
not to be overjoyed
at this day?
  (Basil the Great)

You wanted to be God,
although you were human,
and so you were lost.
He wanted to be human.
although he was God,
so that he could look
for what was lost.
Your human pride
struck you down
with such a force
that only the humanity of God
could make you rise up again.
   (Augustine)

Child, dear child,
help me to discover
even in the most earnest
and the most severe people
the child asleep in their hearts.
   (Dom Helder Camara)

Our desire is that the light of Jesus will shine <u>everywhere</u> in the city—and we are so deeply grateful for the encouragement and prayer we receive from so many of you.

Peace and Joy this Christmas

POSTSCRIPT:
A SON'S PERSPECTIVE

Dr. Peter "Pete" Bylsma

Bud passed peacefully into the next stage of his life during his sleep the morning of May 12, 2021 at an adult family home in Kirkland, Washington. He had turned 93 a few weeks before and had been in hospice status for three months due to failing kidneys and cancer in his bladder that had spread to other areas. He was so happy he was finally going to see Jesus and many of his friends who were in heaven. He knew Patti would be in good hands once he departed this earth – his four children would make sure she was well cared for. He also wanted me to published his memoirs, and as I was just about to publish _The Short Bible_ through WestBow Press in early 2021, I knew I could get it done rather quickly. As of the fall of 2022, Patti was still living at an adult family, a short drive from our home.

Bud was buried in the Psalms section of Abbey View Memorial Park in Brier, Washington. A short gravesite service celebrating his life took place on June 1, 2021. (The order of service and the scriptures read are provided after the eulogy below.) Many family members, including Patti and my two brothers, and friends from his days in Young Life, at Bethany Presbyterian Church, and other ministries were able to attend due to relaxed COVID-19 restrictions. Many stories were shared about Bud's life, his character, and the impact he had on individuals. An online search of his name will identify obituaries that have been posted in various places. Pictures and memories are posted on the Dignity Memorial website for its Bothell location *(www. dignitymemorial.com/obituaries/bothell-wa)*.

His memoirs recorded his life until he was 80 years old. He continued to teach Bible studies in his retirement home, provide guidance and support to various churches and non-profit ministries, and mentor individuals with whom he had a strong connection. At the memorial service, I shared the following eulogy about Bud (dad).

* * * * * * * * * *

Eulogy

Norman, Bud, Dad, Uncle Bud, or Grandpa – he went by many names and had many roles, and his family name was usually butchered: Blysma, Bills-ma, Ba-LIZ-ma, Buy-AL-zma. (He had a sense of humor, but never at the expense of others, and sometimes he called himself Blood Plasma). But when you hear the name Bud Bylsma, those who knew him know how to say it right and will never forget him.

I'm going to take a few minutes to give you my reflections of dad – who he was and what he did for others. But my words will be inadequate – to really know all aspects of his life, you need to talk to others and read his memoirs when I get them published in a few months.

Dad was multidimensional and lived an uncommon life. He was both **mischievous** and **smart**, and was both from day one. We have been told how he was caught stealing milk from his twin brother Pat. They shared a crib, and when they got their milk bottles, dad would drink his and then take Pat's from him, but he would give his empty bottle to Pat, so it looked like both of them were fed. It's no coincidence that Bud ended up being bigger and stronger than Pat. While he had a genius IQ, he didn't get good grades in high school (only a couple A's), and he barely graduated from college. He didn't like going to class, preferring instead to work and play basketball.

He was raised in a conservative and strict Dutch family during the depression. This meant he was always very **frugal.** This quality came in handy – he became very creative with his money and learned to work hard, often holding multiple jobs at a time in high school and college. It seemed like he was never *not* working in some way. He would cut corners to meet his goals, and he would cut through alleys and parking lots at a fast pace if he could save 30 seconds and a nickel on gas. (I confess that I also do this to some extent, so I guess it's hereditary.) Although he owned about 70 cars during his lifetime, he didn't know how to fix them. He bargained hard to get a good used car at a discount and owned them until they were going to need some kind of major work. Putting in oil and gas was about all he did. Then he would sell the car for about the same amount he bought it for. Riding shotgun with him was like riding on a roller coaster – I think his turn signal stopped working from a lack of use. He blew through stop signs if nobody was around. (We convinced him to give up driving last November.)

He didn't make much money at any time during his life. From a financial point of view, we were impoverished in his early Young Life years. But we didn't know it because he and mom trusted God to take care of us, and they never complained or talked about it. He and mom held a couple family meetings when we were older, and he would explain our financial situation. We were all stunned. I once asked him, "Dad, are we poor?" He replied, "No, we're not poor. We just don't have much money." But he never considered the salary level when thinking about taking a new job – he wanted to make a difference in people's lives – that would make him happy and fulfilled, and the money we needed to survive would come from somewhere. (The handout about Divine Interventions has a couple examples of when this happened.)

Being Dutch, he was also very **stubborn**. Once he had a point of view on something, he was not shy about sharing it, and it seemed impossible to change his mind if you disagreed. He didn't like it when somebody disagreed with him, but he might change his mind later after reflecting on the conversation. He did compromise when he had to, and I saw him shift politically from being slightly right of center, then shift to the left, then back to the right. In the past few years, he was left of center. The unusual teachings of the gospel influenced his political views, and he was very concerned about where the white evangelical church in America was heading these days.

He liked to have fun, and Young Life was a perfect fit for him. His career lasted 30 years as he rose to national prominence in an organization that was furthering the Kingdom of God but didn't pay their staff very well. He bought the cheapest house he could find in a very wealthy suburb of Chicago (Hinsdale), and we went to good schools while he rubbed shoulders with many executives who taught him about management and leadership. He became close friends with key Christian leaders in Chicago who taught him about the many types of economic and social injustices that occurred there.

Most people retire after working 30 years in the same organization, but dad was just getting started, proving you **can** teach an old dog new tricks. The next 35 years of full-time ministry were entirely different. His move to Bangladesh at age 53 taught him so much. He knew nothing about the kind of work he led there, so he studied how to develop and inspire people in new ways in this new context. He realized that people's bodies and emotions were just as important as their spirit. He hadn't learned much about economics or politics, but living in Bangladesh changed his perspectives on those topics. Living there also made his driving even worse, but he really enjoyed driving like a maniac and not having to worry about getting a ticket.

When he returned home, his heart had become closest to those who were disadvantaged in some way – the homeless, single moms, refugees, the poor, the poor in spirit. He met regularly with a number of black pastors in the Rainier Valley (the south part of Seattle) to encourage them in their ministries. He was their "boy" and loved being the only white guy in the room. He got to know a homeless woman and visited her in prison after she murdered her female lover. Then he paid for her train ticket to the east coast after she got out so she could live with some friends. (He also helped her get back on the right train after she got off in the Midwest and was left behind and called him frantically.) Many stories can be told about such generosity, so he could be very generous while also being frugal. He continued to mentor and teach others into his 90s. Some of you are here today because of that, and he has been like a second father or grandfather to many.

In the end, he was **wise and driven to be relevant**. He never stopped trying to help people understand how wonderful Jesus was. He led Bible studies at their retirement home until about a year ago. Last year when COVID started to hit the country, he and I sat in the emergency room at Evergreen Hospital in Kirkland, where COVID patients were starting to die, and we waited together for him to be seen about severe pains he was having. I was planning to write a book that summarized the Bible, and I wanted his perspective on the key points of the Scriptures. As we sat together for three hours, I asked him many questions, and he gave me the details on the big picture – that a loving God wanted a relationship with human beings, and that individuals and those who follow Jesus should demonstrate love to others in extravagant ways. He read the story of the prodigal son as a story about a prodigal father – lavishness in honoring those who don't deserve it. It's all about love, not about doing certain things or not doing certain things.

He was always **thinking, often in new and creative ways.** He was always **learning**, **strategizing**, **teaching**, and **serving**. He was a **pioneer,** not a settler. Like Jesus, he had unique ways of communicating. His writing style was unorthodox and engaging, and he told unusual stories or analogies to make a theological point. We have heard many unique one-liners.

- *Never let school get in the way of your education.*
- *A Christian is somebody who turns out to be one.*
- *All truth is God's truth.*
- *Communication is not what is said but what is heard.*
- *Evangelism is one beggar telling another beggar where to find bread.*

My favorite analogy was how he defined grace, as he contrasted it with justice and mercy.

> **Justice** is where you appear before a judge for breaking the law, and the judge says, "guilty, pay $250. **Mercy** is when the judge says, "guilty, but you don't have to pay the $250 fine." **Grace** is when the judge says, "guilty, here's $250."

He never said this explicitly, but his life's motto could be summed up in this way: **Become aware of the needs of others, and when you understand their needs, be creative and find a way to do what is necessary to help them in a way that supports and maintains their dignity.**

He relaxed by reading and watching golf and basketball, and he and we three boys had lots of fun golfing together. He was always saying "nuts" or "bad words" when he hit a bad shot, which was often. When we got together as adults, we mainly played cards and put together puzzles at some remote vacation site. Dad was especially good at playing bridge and doing sudoku puzzles. He had a sweet tooth, especially for ice cream and M&Ms. He tipped the staff at the retirement home with bags of candy. About a year ago, he read that drinking red wine and eating dark chocolate would lengthen a person's life, and he wanted to start consuming both. I told him it was a little late for them to have much effect on him, but I still gave both to him. He only ate the chocolate (I don't think he knew how to open the bottle of wine).

He liked to tell funny stories, often with a theological twist. One time he told me a story about two men who were close friends and played baseball together. One of them died, went to heaven, then came back to earth to visit his friend. His friend asked him if there is baseball in heaven. He said he had good news and bad news. The good news was that there was baseball in heaven; the bad news was that his friend was scheduled to be the starting pitcher the next day. If there's baseball in heaven, I'm sure basketball is played there, too. Dad is probably up there now, organizing a league and trying to identify somebody who would be a good commissioner. But dad, just remember that Jesus knows all your tricks (like holding the bottom of the pants of the guy in front of you so they won't jump, which lets you get the rebound)—the refs in heaven are probably going to call fouls on you.

A lot of dad rubbed off on me, and I owe much of my success in life to him. I was honored to be close to him and live close by in his final years. He told me more than once that he was ready to "graduate." God used him in unusual ways here on earth, and we all will miss him very much.

Let me finish by honoring mom, Patti Bylsma. Our family frequently moved as dad took on more responsibility in Young Life. The moves helped make us kids adaptable to change, but they also deprived us of life-long friendships. I lived in eight cities by the time I was 16. Dad's devotion to relational evangelism meant he was often away from home, and when he

was home, he was often preoccupied in thought or reading as he prepared for his next meeting or talk. So mom ran things on the home front, giving up her own career aspirations to take care of us four kids, which she had before she turned 30. She faithfully stood by Bud for nearly 71 years of marriage, proving to all of us who knew dad well that she was a true saint. She went back to school and got her BA from Biola at age 44 and had straight A's while still being a mom of four kids at home in Orange County, CA. She went on to specialize in teaching English to non-English speakers, and she taught teachers of English in many countries about how best to teach English to their students. She literally walked in the valley of death without fear to start a tutoring program in the most dangerous part of Chicago (Cabrini Green). She also was involved in various prayer ministries. If my parents were a cake, dad was the icing while mom was the flour and yeast – unseen but very active behind the scenes. Dad couldn't have done anything without her. Let's give her a round of applause!

With that, I invite my "little" brother Phil to come up and say a few words. After he speaks, other members of the family are welcome to speak, and then everybody else will be given a chance to say a few words, starting with Pastor Hossain, the Executive Director from HEED Bangladesh.

Celebrating the Life of
Norman M. "Bud" Bylsma
June 1, 2021 10:00 am
Abbey View Memorial Park
Brier, WA

*(please wear a mask and practice social distancing
if you have not been fully vaccinated)*

Welcome & Introductions   Pete Bylsma, oldest son

Prayer   Anne Lider, close friend

Scripture Reading   Kurt Campbell, close friend

Remembering Bud – A Son's Perspective   Pete Bylsma

The Family Remembers

The Audience Remembers

Saying Goodbye to Bud

"My Tribute – To God Be the Glory" (Andrae Crouch)
Sung by Pastor Harvey Drake, Emerald City Bible Fellowship

Closing Remarks

Scripture Shared at Bud's Gravesite Service

Ecclesiastes 3: 1-2b, 4
There is a time for everything, and a season for every activity under the heavens: a time to be born and a time to die, a time to weep and a time to laugh, a time to mourn and a time to dance.

John 11:25
Jesus said, "I am the resurrection and the life. The one who believes in me will live, even though they die."

John 14: 1-3
Do not let your hearts be troubled. You believe in God; believe also in me. My Father's house has many rooms; if that were not so, would I have told you that I am going there to prepare a place for you? And if I go and prepare a place for you, I will come back and take you to be with me that you also may be where I am.

Romans 8:35, 37-39
Who shall separate us from the love of Christ? Shall trouble or hardship or persecution or famine or nakedness or danger or sword? No, in all these things we are more than conquerors through him who loved us. For I am convinced that neither death nor life, neither angels nor demons, neither the present nor the future, nor any powers, neither height nor depth, nor anything else in all creation, will be able to separate us from the love of God that is in Christ Jesus our Lord.

2 Corinthians 4: 16,17
We do not lose heart. Though outwardly we are wasting away, yet inwardly we are being renewed day by day. For our light and momentary troubles are achieving for us an eternal glory that

far outweighs them all. So we fix our eyes not on what is seen, but on what is unseen, since what is seen is temporary, but what is unseen is eternal.

<u>Job 19: 25-27</u>
I know that my redeemer lives, and that in the end he will stand on the earth. And after my skin has been destroyed, yet in my flesh I will see God; I myself will see him with my own eyes. How my heart yearns within me!

<u>Psalm 27: 1, 4</u>
The LORD is my light and my salvation—whom shall I fear? The LORD is the stronghold of my life—of whom shall I be afraid? One thing I ask from the LORD, this only do I seek: that I may dwell in the house of the LORD all the days of my life, to gaze on the beauty of the LORD and to seek him in his temple.

<u>Revelations 21: 1-5</u>
Then I saw a new heaven and a new earth, for the first heaven and the first earth had passed away, and there was no longer any sea. I saw the Holy City, the new Jerusalem, coming down out of heaven from God, prepared as a bride beautifully dressed for her husband. And I heard a loud voice from the throne saying, "Look! God's dwelling place is now among the people, and he will dwell with them. They will be his people, and God himself will be with them and be their God. 'He will wipe every tear from their eyes. There will be no more death' or mourning or crying or pain, for the old order of things has passed away." He who was seated on the throne said, "I am making everything new!"

<u>Philippians 1:21</u>
For me, to live is Christ, and to die is gain.

www.ingramcontent.com/pod-product-compliance
Lightning Source LLC
Chambersburg PA
CBHW020437130626
46549CB00001B/188